EXPECTATIONS

NOTES

including
- *Life of the Author*
- *Brief Summary of the Novel*
- *List of Characters*
- *Summaries and Commentaries*
- *Critical Analysis*
- *Character Analyses*
- *Review Questions*
- *Selected Bibliography*

by
Arnie Jacobson
University of Nebraska

Cliffs Notes

INCORPORATED

LINCOLN, NEBRASKA 68501

Editor

Gary Carey, M.A.
University of Colorado

Consulting Editor

James L. Roberts, Ph.D.
Department of English
University of Nebraska

Cliffs Notes, Inc.   Lincoln, Nebraska

CONTENTS

Great Expectations Notes

LIFE OF THE AUTHOR

Charles Dickens was one of the most successful of English novelists. He was also one of the greatest. And he was certainly one of the least understood.

Precisely because he *was* so successful—in periodicals, in English book editions, and in American editions (which were largely pirated)—he became suspect to the captive force of critics. A man *that* successful couldn't really be *that* good. It bothered no one, except perhaps Dickens, that this was the same thing Elizabethan critics had said about Shakespeare. Like Sir Walter Scott before him, Dickens wrote out of a compulsion to succeed. He had, like Scott, taken on the support of a huge and expensive living establishment. Payment could come from only one place: his pen. But by 1860, the year in which *Great Expectations* was written, the till was beginning to run dry. Even his fantastic success as a public lecturer could not meet his expenses, and his latest book, *The Uncommercial Traveller,* a book of sketches, had only mediocre success. In addition, his magazine, *All the Year Round,* had begun to show a significant drop in sales. Drastic action was called for. This action resulted in *Great Expectations.*

It is no accident that in this time of crisis Dickens reached far back into his own experience and wrote a book about the young man he might have been. Although Pip, the youth in *Great Expectations,* was not completely Charles Dickens, as David Copperfield, his predecessor, had also not been, Dickens had, in the manner of all great artists, plunged into his own soul for the great book he needed, and the novel was an enormous success.

Charles John Huffam Dickens was born in 1812 at Landport, Portsea, which is on the southern coast of England; he was the second of eight children of an Admiralty clerk. At the time of his birth, his family was relatively well-to-do, but his father, like Mr. Micawber in *David Copperfield,* was incapable of managing his own financial affairs. In 1824 he was placed in a debtors' prison in London—symbolized by Newgate in *Great Expectations*—and young Charles was sent to work in a factory. Out of this experience came the roots of Dickens' strong sympathies for the underprivileged.

After his father had been released from prison as a result of receiving a legacy, Charles spent three years in school at

Hampstead. After a couple of years as a law clerk—an experience which also reflects itself in this novel—he entered the newspaper business. His success as a reporter was so spectacular that he abandoned a theatrical career on which he had half launched himself. He was a born actor, as his career as a dramatic reader of his own work testifies. His death in 1870 was a direct result of overstrain during his last lecture tour, ironically in America, a country he never liked and which he had written about in *American Notes* (1842) and *Martin Chuzzlewit* (1844).

In 1836, Dickens married Catherine Hogarth, from whom he was later divorced though her sister remained his companion thereafter; also in that year, he published *Sketches by Boz* and began publication of *The Posthumous Papers of the Pickwick Club,* his first great success. He was now launched as a successful writer, which he continued to be until he died, leaving *The Mystery of Edwin Drood,* his last novel, unfinished. There have been several attempts to complete this book, but none of them have been successful. Dickens took his last secret—how the book would end—to the grave with him.

The character of his work changed radically in his later years. It became deeper, more brooding, and less compromising. Even though he continued his practice of writing for serial publication, he had perfected the technique to the point where in *Great Expectations* the seams between installments are invisible. This later period began with *Bleak House* (1853) and includes the following other major novels: *Little Dorrit* (1857), *A Tale of Two Cities* (1859), *Great Expectations* (1861), and *Our Mutual Friend* (1865). *Our Mutual Friend,* his last completed full-length novel, shows a distinct falling off from *Great Expectations,* the high point of the series and of Dickens' canon.

A major advance in Dickens' work in this last period was his greatly increased sensitivity to language. The style which he had been developing through a long series of novels was now completely under his control; in *Great Expectations* it is one of the glories of the novel. His genius for fusing style, plot, and characterization made *Great Expectations* a masterpiece and Dickens one of the greatest writers who ever lived.

INTRODUCTION TO THE NOVEL

There is general agreement that *Great Expectations* is Dickens' best book. *David Copperfield,* to a considerable extent because of Mr. Micawber, remains a sentimental favorite; *A Tale of Two Cities* is widely used in schools because of its seeming simplicity; *Bleak*

House, a much less read but strong and somber book, has its advocates; and *A Christmas Carol* arrives promptly on schedule every Christmas. Yet it is always to *Great Expectations* that one returns if one wishes to reread Dickens and recapture the experience that one encounters in the presence of genius.

To explain why *Great Expectations* is Dickens' finest novel, it is necessary to study his plot structure, his style, and his thematic elements, which is done in the Critical Analysis section of these Notes. Of equal importance to an understanding of Dickens is a keen attention to his characters. With the exception of Faulkner, Dickens probably created more memorable characters than any other novelist in English literature; despite the handicap of writing for serial publication, he regularly constructed plots which keep the reader's attention to the end; he became the master of a unique personal style which was ideally suited to his purposes, which is immediately recognizable, and which has never been imitated; his imagination was prodigious; and he used all these gifts to present, in story after story, the ancient theme of the struggle between good and evil. We can add one more. Dickens' books are adhesive: they stick in the mind long after the reader has finished them. This is perhaps one of the best tests of a great writer.

As an example of Dickens' uncompromising skill as a novelist, consider the way in which he develops the book's basic irony: the fact that Pip's money and great expectations, and his illusory and aristocratic love both stem from the same source—Magwitch, his benefactor and Estella's father. This amazing coincidence violates nothing that has gone before; it is consistent with everything that has happened since the first chapter. Dickens carefully drops hints along the way, events which become significant only in retrospect, so that when the truth finally dawns on Pip (in Chapters 48 and 50) it is completely plausible. Futhermore, Dickens uses this—without comment—as a symbol of the thematic idea that wealth and position are corrupting and corrupt.

Great Expectations is a well-structured novel in another way. In the character of Pip, Dickens makes a serious effort to present the *ambivalence* of the problem of good and evil. Pip is not simply a young man of native goodness thrown on adversity but finally rising above it. He is a complicated mixture of good and bad—considerate and selfish, loving and callous, humble and ambitious, honest and self-deceiving. The core of Dickens' universal theme lies inside Pip himself, and the triumph of good comes about through Pip's self-discovery.

Even this is ambivalent. Pip's self-discovery is forced on him, primarily by Magwitch. In this murderer and lifelong criminal Pip discovers a genuine goodness which finally breaks through his wall of selfishness. Even at this point, however, he continues to act uncertainly. Having first refused to accept any more of the convict's money out of loathing for him, he continues to refuse out of what he considers nobility when loathing turns to love. The net result is that he deprives Magwitch of his one great wish in life, though he is considerate enough not to let him know it, and makes certain that all the money that the convict has worked so hard to amass for Pip's benefit will be confiscated by the courts.

In Pip's character development, the complexity of the struggle between good and evil is continuously demonstrated. Even in his triumph there is loss: he finds himself, but at a cost, not simply of money but in a crippling of his emotional life. He never marries, getting his family life indirectly through Herbert and Clara, and he finally achieves success through his own efforts, in partnership with Herbert and Clarriker in the counting house, but there is no evidence that he takes any great satisfaction in it.

There is genuine art at work here, as there is in the creation of the other characters, in the plot structure, and in the style. All of these elements are directly related to the developments within Pip, which are the core of the book. This is the fusion which, when applied to material of the magnitude and significance Dickens offers here, is the hallmark of a true work of art.

BRIEF SUMMARY OF THE NOVEL

Pip, an orphan, lives with his sister and her husband, Joe Gargery, the village blacksmith. One day on the marshes he meets an escaped convict who forces him to steal food and a file from the Gargerys. The convict is almost immediately recaptured. Pip is subsequently hired by Miss Havisham, a wealthy, elderly recluse, as a playmate for her beautiful, haughty, adopted daughter, Estella, with whom he immediately falls in love.

When Jaggers, a shrewd and powerful lawyer, tells him that money has been settled on him and that he has "great expectations," Pip assumes that Miss Havisham is his benefactor. In London, where Jaggers is his guardian, and Jaggers' assistant, Wemmick, becomes his friend, Pip learns gentlemanly manners from his roommate, Herbert Pocket, a relative of Miss Havisham's, and with Herbert's father he begins his education. He persuades himself that Miss Havisham is preparing him to marry Estella. Meanwhile, he neglects Joe, his earliest and best friend, and also Biddy, a girl who has helped him and the Gargerys; in short, he becomes somewhat of a snob.

One stormy evening when he is twenty-three, a weather-beaten stranger appears at his door. Pip recognizes him as "his convict" and is horrified to learn that this is his benefactor. Magwitch has been exiled to New South Wales, Australia, has made money, and has now returned to England, despite penalty of death, to see Pip. What has sustained him in the long years "down under" has been his determination to repay Pip's boyhood kindness by making him a gentleman. Revolted, Pip nevertheless feels obligated to help Magwitch. As a further blow, he learns that Estella is to marry Drummle, a boor.

On Wemmick's advice, Pip and Herbert move Magwitch to a house by the river. In quick succession, Pip saves Miss Havisham from fire, though she later dies; discovers that Magwitch is Estella's father; is almost murdered by Orlick, Joe's former assistant; and attempts to get Magwitch on a boat headed for the continent and safety.

Magwitch is captured but dies before his execution from injuries sustained in an underwater struggle with his old enemy, Compeyson, who brought about his capture. Pip, who has learned both love and humility from Magwitch, falls seriously ill and is nursed back to health by Joe. His false pride gone, Pip joins Herbert in business in India. Years later he again sees Estella, also educated by suffering. In the original ending they part friends; in the revised ending they will stay together.

LIST OF CHARACTERS

Pip (Philip Pirrip)

The narrator and chief character of the novel has been an orphan since infancy. His driving ambition is to better his station in life; unfortunately, Pip rejects his closest friends in order to achieve his social goals, and it is only after much heartbreak and disappointment that he realizes that good friends are far more valuable than wealth.

Miss Havisham

She is an eccentric lady who lives in semi-seclusion with her adopted daughter, Estella. Because she was deserted on her wedding day, she has reared Estella to take malicious revenge on the male sex.

Joe Gargery

As Pip's brother-in-law and father-figure, Joe is the most sympathetic of all the characters in this book. He is a hard worker, a loyal and gentle friend, and a highly moral man.

Abel Magwitch

Pip's benefactor, a convict, was deeply grateful when young Pip supplied him with food and a file after he attempted to escape. He worked many years in New South Wales, Australia, to amass enough money so that he could give the lad a better chance in life than he had.

Estella Havisham

As the adopted daughter of the bitter, eccentric Miss Havisham, she was brought up as an instrument of her benefactress' revenge on men. She is both beautiful and poised, and Pip is infatuated with these qualities, despite the fact that she openly scorns him.

Molly

Mr. Jaggers' housekeeper; the true mother of Estella by Magwitch.

Mr. Jaggers

The Old Bailey lawyer who defended Magwitch; he is commissioned by Magwitch to see that Pip is given an allowance at the proper time and made a gentleman, without Pip's knowledge of who his benefactor is. During this time, Jaggers acts as Pip's guardian.

Uncle Pumblechook

A pompous seed merchant; Joe's uncle. He is one of the sharpest expressions of Dickens' unrelenting scorn of humbug and hypocrisy.

John Wemmick

Mr. Jaggers' chief clerk has two life-styles: at the office, he is a piece of legal machinery, but at home he is an eccentric romantic, devising ever-new gadgets for his mini-castle home. He shows unusual patience and love for his deaf father, whom he calls the "Aged P."

Mr. Wopsle

He would have liked to be a clergyman, but since he was not of the right social class, he became a parish lay clerk until frustration lured him to small town theatrical stages.

Mrs. Joe

Joe's wife was more than twenty years old when Pip was born. She reared him "by hand," meaning basically that she hand-fed him as a baby, but as he grew older, she used a large and heavy hand to discipline him. Her temper proves her undoing when Orlick, her husband's apprentice, retaliates and almost murders her.

Biddy

Like Pip, Biddy is also an orphan. She is good-hearted, wise, and sympathetic to Pip's troubles. Early in the novel, she has a romantic crush on young Pip, but eventually she falls in love with and marries Joe Gargery.

Orlick

An employee of Joe Gargery and one of Pip's enemies. Orlick is broad-shouldered, strong and swarthy, and has a sharp, vicious temper. His attack on Mrs. Joe leaves her paralyzed and virtually speechless.

Compeyson

Miss Havisham's gentlemanly scoundrel-fiancé. He exploits her and her brother, then deserts her on her wedding day.

Herbert Pocket

Initially, Pip takes a dislike to this "pale young gentleman"; later, however, the two become close friends. Herbert is an amiable and frank person, easy to get along with, and a hard worker.

Bentley Drummle

Pip's rival for Estella's affections. A sturdy, heavy-set man, he is proud and chronically ill at ease. Estella marries him for his social position and wealth. Despite Drummle's unsympathetic qualities, he is highly instrumental in humanizing Estella.

Mr. Wopsle's Great-Aunt

She conducts the school and the store in which Biddy works.

Mr. Hubble

The wheelwright in Pip's village.

Mr. Trabb

The local tailor and undertaker.

Trabb's Boy

Pip's old enemy who nevertheless guides Herbert and Startop when Orlick is about to murder Pip.

Sarah Pocket, Georgiana Pocket, Mr. Raymond, and Mrs. Camilla

The toady relatives of Miss Havisham who have vain expectations.

Matthew Pocket

Herbert's father and the sole member of the family who will not condescend to flatter Miss Havisham; he is also an ineffectual father and a celebrated author and lecturer on family problems.

Mrs. Pocket

His wife; a studious reader of books on peerage.

Flopson and Millers

Nurses at the Pockets.

Mrs. Collier

A pretentious neighbor of the Pockets.

Startop

A former roomer at the Pockets, along with Pip and Drummle, who helps Pip and Herbert attempt Magwitch's escape.

The Avenger

A young, useless servant whom Pip, in his days as a professional gentleman, employs.

Bill Barley

An ex-purser; father of Herbert Pocket's fiancée and eventual wife.

Clara Barley

His devoted, sensible daughter, whom Herbert marries.

Mrs. Whimple

Landlady to the Barleys and friend and confidante of Herbert and Clara.

The Aged P.

John Wemmick's father.

Miss Skiffins

John Wemmick's bride.

Mr. Skiffins

Accountant and her brother; he arranges the business of Herbert's partnership with Clarriker.

Clarriker

A merchant.

SUMMARIES AND COMMENTARIES

CHAPTERS 1-6

Summary

Pip, a seven-year-old orphan whose real name is Philip Pirrip, lives with his sister, Mrs. Joe Gargery, wife of the village blacksmith. Their home is in the marsh country, down by the river and close to the sea. His parents, whom Pip has never seen, are buried in a graveyard in the marshes, along with five little brothers. Pip often visits the graves, his only momento of his family.

On one such visit, one bleak Christmas Eve, he is surprised by "a fearful man, all in coarse gray, with a great iron on his leg," who rises from among the graves. After turning Pip upside down to empty his pockets and finding only a piece of bread, the man quizzes him and finds out that Joe, Pip's guardian, is a blacksmith. He demands that early next morning, Pip bring him a file and some "wittles" (food) or he'll have Pip's "heart and liver out." To further terrify the boy, he adds that he has a young man with him who "has a secret way pecooliar to himself, of getting at a boy, and at his heart, and at his liver."

After swearing that he will be there, Pip flees in terror, and the man, hugging himself to keep warm, limps down toward the river, where a gibbet (gallows) stands outlined in the dusk.

Arriving home, Pip finds that his sister Georgiana, a stern woman with a heavy hand which she uses freely on both Pip and Joe, is out looking for him. "She made a grab at Tickler," Joe says, "and she ram-paged [rampaged] out." On returning, she freely applies Tickler, a wax-ended piece of cane, to Pip's behind; then, in her usual aggressive way, she serves Pip and Joe some bread and butter. Pip, mindful of his need to collect "wittles," slips his slice of bread down his pants leg. Joe, a good, gentle man, fears that Pip has swallowed it in one bite, whereupon Mrs. Joe drags Pip away for a dose of tar-water.

Since it is Christmas Eve, Pip has many chores to do, and as he finishes, he hears the sounds of large guns. He learns that this means that a convict has escaped from the Hulks, the prison ships lying just off the marshes. Another convict escaped yesterday, Joe says. Sent to bed, Pip is too frightened to sleep, and at dawn, he goes down to rob the pantry. It is well stocked because of the season, and he manages to steal bread, cheese, mincemeat, some brandy from a stone jug which he replenishes from a kitchen jug, a meat bone with very little on it, and "a beautiful round pork pie."

He appropriates a file from Joe's forge, adjacent to the kitchen, then runs for the marshes.

Racing through the misty morning, Pip sees the convict seated in the marshes with his back to him. Touching him on the shoulder, Pip finds, to his horror, that this is another man, dressed in similar clothing, complete with leg-iron. The man takes a futile swing at Pip and disappears in the mist. Convinced that he has seen the fearsome "young man" described by "his convict," Pip hurries on to the appointed place.

While "his convict" wolfs down the food, Pip asks apologetically whether he should not save some for the young man, whom he has just seen. The convict, much agitated, grasps Pip roughly. "Where?" he says. "Over there. . . . Didn't you hear the cannon last night?" Pip asks. "When a man's alone on these flats," the convict replies, "with a light head and a light stomach, perishing of cold and want, he hears nothin' all night but guns firing and voices calling."

Learning that the other man has a bruise on his left cheek, the convict shouts, "Show me the way he went. I'll pull him down, like a bloodhound." He grabs the file and begins to work frenziedly on his leg-iron. Pip, seeing that he is ignored, slips away for home.

Mrs. Joe's Christmas greeting to Pip is "And where the deuce ha' *you* been?" Pip, expecting the constable to arrive immediately, explains that he has been to hear the carols. He and Joe sit down to a breakfast of bread and milk. Mrs. Joe, having planned a superb dinner, has too much to do to bother with a decent breakfast for them. She is also too busy with cleaning to go to church, and so Joe and Pip represent the family. Joe is uncomfortable in his "holiday clothes," and Pip is in a torment of fear and remorse about his theft, particularly the pork pie.

The dinner guests arrive: Mr. Wopsle, the church clerk; Mr. Hubble, the wheelwright, and his wife; and Joe's Uncle Pumblechook, a well-to-do seed merchant in a nearby town. Uncle Pumblechook brings his perennial gift, a bottle of sherry and a bottle of port, and Mrs. Joe receives them with her usual deference to Pumblechook.

At dinner, Pip gets the worst servings, accompanied by sermons on his character by the entire company except for Joe, who tries to compensate by repeatedly giving him more gravy. As the climax of the dinner, Mrs. Joe goes out to get the pork pie. Pip, knowing that the pie has long since been devoured, rushes to the door—only to be met by a party of soldiers, one of whom holds out a pair of handcuffs.

Pip's secret dealings with the convict are safe, however; the sergeant merely wants the handcuffs repaired. When Joe is finished, he and the soldiers set off for the marshes in search of the convicts, accompanied by Mr. Wopsle and Pip, Mrs. Joe having given her permission out of curiosity to find out what happens. As they approach the Battery, where Pip had given his convict the "wittles" and the file, they hear several loud shouts and find the two convicts locked in a desperate struggle at the bottom of a ditch.

Pip's convict explains that he was dragging the other man, whom he obviously loathes, back to the Hulks. The second convict says he was being murdered. The sergeant replies that it makes little difference, and they set off for the landing-place. Pip's convict, to whom Pip has been able to give an indication that he was not responsible for the capture, announces that he stole food from Joe's house, including the pork pie which Mrs. Joe missed just as the soldiers arrived. Joe assures him that he is welcome to it. The boats then return the convicts to the Hulks.

Pip is miserable over not telling Joe about what he has done, but he is afraid of losing Joe's confidence and friendship. "In a word, I was too cowardly to do what I knew to be right, as I had been too cowardly to avoid doing what I knew to be wrong."

Joe carries the sleepy boy home on his back, and Pip gets the usual gruff reception from his sister and Mr. Pumblechook, who has an ingenious theory about how the convict got in the house and stole the pork pie.

Commentary

Dickens begins this novel boldly: a sad little orphan is confronted in a cemetery by an escaped convict; already on page two, we hear Pip cry, "Don't cut my throat, sir!" There are no long paragraphs of exposition, of setting, or character development, as other writers often used at that time. Dickens sketched in a few strokes, suggesting the desolation of the setting, gained our sympathy by having his main character a young orphan, and launched into his story.

He wrote this novel in monthly installments, for his own magazine, *All the Year Round*, and wanted to capture an audience. He did. From the first chapters, *Great Expectations* was a success and bolstered the magazine and Dickens' fame.

The novel is introduced as a remembrance, as a memoir, which adds authenticity to the story; it involves the reader through identification and creates curiosity as to the fate of young Pip, the orphan. Immediately, we feel sympathy for Pip because he has no parents and is standing before their graves; but, more important, Dickens makes us feel sympathy for Pip and Joe because both of them are, in a sense, victims or "prisoners" of Mrs. Joe's temper. Thus he creates a subtle parallel between Pip, a victim of misfortune and his sister's violence, and the escaped prisoner, another victim of circumstances—a figure of pity as well as horror.

Of particular importance in these first chapters is the emphasis which Dickens puts on the bond between Joe and Pip. Because both of them must yield and succumb to Mrs. Joe's fierceness, they form a special sensitiveness toward one another. Later, when Pip is tempted by ambition and the promise of "great expectations," he will, with much guilt, sever this bond with Joe, a "mere blacksmith."

Take note in this section of Dickens' plotting. The escaped convict needs a file to cut his leg-irons. Pip mentions that his brother-in-law is a blacksmith. Blacksmiths have files. This is coincidence, but a coincidence that is cleverly calculated by Dickens. From Pip's fear and his natural generosity, he aids the convict, an act which will affect Pip's whole future.

CHAPTERS 7-13

Summary

Pip, who is to be apprenticed to Joe when he is old enough, attends an evening school run by Mr. Wopsle's great-aunt, but unfortunately she sleeps through her own classes. One evening, about a year after the convict was recaptured, Pip shows Joe a badly misspelled letter which he has spent an hour or two working on. Joe is much impressed, although he can do no more than pick out the letters *J* and *O*, for Joe himself is illiterate. Pip then decides to secretly teach Joe to read.

Mrs. Joe arrives after a marketing trip with Uncle Pumblechook, and they announce that Pip has been asked to go and "play" at the house of Miss Havisham, a rich and grim woman who lives in seclusion in a large, dismal house in the town. Pip is vigorously scrubbed and dressed, then he sets off to spend the night with Uncle Pumblechook before going to Miss Havisham's. He is greatly puzzled about *why* he will play for her and *what* he will play.

After a breakfast at which Pumblechook examines Pip interminably on arithmetic, they set out for Miss Havisham's Satis House. At the locked gate, Pip is admitted by a condescending young girl who rudely turns Pumblechook away. Then, in a room where no daylight enters, Pip encounters Miss Havisham, a fantastic character dressed in a yellowed bridal gown which hangs loosely over her skeletal figure. She tells Pip that she has not seen the sun since before he was born, that she has a broken heart, and that she wishes him to "play" for her diversion. She then orders him to call Estella, the girl who admitted him, and directs them to play cards. As they begin the only game Pip knows, "Beggar My Neighbour," Pip realizes that everything in this room stopped all at once, a long time ago. Estella, disdainfully noting Pip's coarse hands and thick boots, ridicules him and "beggars" (defeats) him thoroughly.

Afterward, Miss Havisham tells Pip to come back in six days, and Estella leads him out and gives him bread and meat and beer "as insolently as if I were a dog in disgrace." As he leaves, Pip has a momentary vision of a figure much like Miss Havisham, hanging from a beam and desperately trying to call to him.

Arriving home, Pip is convinced that to describe things as he saw them would be misunderstood; thus, he launches into a wild series of improvisations, including stories about a black velvet coach, four immense dogs fighting over veal cutlets from a silver platter, and a game with flags. Pip's listeners are suitably impressed. Later, however, Pip sneaks out to the forge, tells Joe that it was all lies, and explains what really happened. Joe, though saddened, advises Pip not to say anything about it to his sister and to tell no more lies in the future. Pip then reflects upon what Estella has said: how "common" his boots and his hands are, and how "common" he himself is.

Next day, Pip decides to make himself "uncommon" and asks Biddy, also an orphan, to secretly help him with his learning. Later, when Pip joins Joe at the Three Jolly Bargemen, he meets a "secret-looking" stranger who asks him many questions and stirs his drink not with a spoon, but with a file—Joe's file. When they are leaving, he gives Pip a bright new shilling wrapped in paper. At home, Mrs. Joe discovers that the "wrapping" is two one-pound notes.

On his second visit to Miss Havisham's, Pip is taken into a large, dusty, once-handsome room. There, on a table covered with rotting cloth is a strange centerpiece, so overhung with cobwebs and spiders that it is impossible to tell what it was. In this room, Miss Havisham tells Pip, is the table where she will be laid out when she is dead; the cobwebbed centerpiece is her wedding cake. Pip then meets several of Miss Havisham's cousins, and he and Estella play cards, after which he has a brief scuffle with a bookish young man. Impressed and delighted, Estella lets Pip kiss her cheek before he leaves.

For the next eight or ten months, Pip returns to Miss Havisham's every other day at noon, pushing her around the rooms in a wheelchair, and playing cards with Estella, who is alternately indifferent, condescending, friendly, and hateful. Miss Havisham questions Pip about his life, but never offers aid in his education or money for his services. At home, speculations about his prospects are never-ending.

One day, Miss Havisham tells Pip to bring Joe to Satis House. It is time, she says, for Pip to become apprenticed to him. Uncomfortably dressed in his Sunday suit, Joe accompanies Pip to Miss Havisham's, and there she establishes the fact that Pip has shown no objection to apprenticeship and that the indenture papers are in order. She then gives Pip a bag containing twenty-five guineas, specifying that this is all he will get for his services. She tells Pip that he is not to come again: "Gargery is your master now."

At Pumblechook's, Joe lies about Miss Havisham's sending regards and money to Mrs. Joe and, after some teasing, he hands over the money. Pip is then formally indentured at Town Hall, and Mrs. Joe treats them all, as well as the Hubbles and Mr. Wopsle, to dinner at the Blue Boar—with Pip's money. Pip, kept awake during the festivities to "enjoy himself," falls asleep at last with the unhappy knowledge that once long ago he liked Joe's trade, but, unfortunately, "once was not now."

Commentary

These chapters show us in detail Pip's growing dislike of his "commonness." Pip should be, one might think, grateful that his sister has taken him in and provided him with food and clothing, but, we discover, Pip has a dreamer's spirit and drive. He is tempted, from the first, by Miss Havisham's rich if eccentric furnishings and by Estella's contemptuous behavior. There is a certain perverseness in Miss Havisham's enjoying Pip's discomfort as he plays cards with the haughty, sharp-tongued Estella, but, because of his feelings of inferiority, Pip is determined that he will learn to read and write and better himself. He is a fiercely determined boy, convinced that someday he will be Estella's cultural equal.

Besides providing us with Pip's growing ambitions and his expectations for a better life than that of a blacksmith, Dickens inserts a key scene in the Three Jolly Bargemen. We realize that Pip's encounter with the escaped convict will indeed have consequences which he—and we—cannot yet imagine. The file which Pip gave to the convict is used to stir a drink, and, in addition, Pip is given money. Earlier, Pip had a nightmare about the reappearance of the file; the dream has come true—and will appear again.

As these chapters end, Pip is alone in his bedroom, unable to sleep. He is miserable, aching for a better position in the world. He does not realize the sick dimensions of Miss Havisham's life, nor has he fathomed the cause and depth of Estella's snobbery. As he was a victim of Mrs. Joe's temper, he is now a victim of social class feelings.

CHAPTERS 14-17

Summary

Home life has never been pleasant for Pip, even though Joe has done his best to make it so, but now it seems "all coarse and common," thanks to Miss Havisham and Estella. Pip would like to run away but does not because Joe has always been good and loyal to him. His greatest fear is that Estella might see him at work and jeer at him.

One day, at his and Joe's favorite retreat down by the Battery, Pip broaches the idea of his paying Miss Havisham a visit (an excuse to see Estella). Joe is against it: when Miss Havisham dismissed Pip, she said that was *all*. Pip argues, and Joe finally acquiesces on the condition that it be merely an expression of gratitude which, if not well received, will not be repeated. For this purpose, Pip asks for a half-holiday.

Next day, Sarah Pocket, a Havisham cousin admits Pip to Satis House. Miss Havisham is alone, with everything unchanged. When Pip tells her he has come only to see how she is and thank her for her help, she invites him back on his birthday. Estella is abroad, she says, "educating for a lady." Shortly after, Pip meets Mr. Wopsle, and as they are going homeward in the misty night, they find the doors of the Jolly Bargemen wide open and the customers in a state of great commotion. Something dreadful has happened at Pip's house while Joe was out: someone, presumably a convict, has broken in, and somebody is injured. The somebody is Mrs. Joe, whom Pip finds lying senseless in front of the fire, felled by a tremendous blow on the back of her head, "destined never to be on the rampage again while she was the wife of Joe."

Found beside Mrs. Joe is a convict's leg-iron, which has clearly been filed off some time ago; both Joe and the people from the Hulks agree on this point. Guiltily, Pip thinks it must be "his convict's" leg-iron.

When Mrs. Joe recovers from the attack, her vision and hearing are impaired and her speech is unintelligible. Her writing, always bad, is a poor means of communication, but her temper is much improved. The problem she has left is the care of the household; the new one she has created is the need for somebody to care for her. Both are solved when Mr. Wopsle's great-aunt dies and Biddy becomes a member of the household. It is Biddy who deduces that a curious "T" which Mrs. Joe is constantly drawing might be a hammer and might refer to Orlick, a surly employee of Joe's. When Orlick is produced, however, Mrs. Joe is very friendly, almost subservient to him. The mystery remains.

Pip's life as an apprentice is disturbed only by his annual visits to Miss Havisham, who gives him a guinea each birthday and a glimpse into her "uncommon" world, enough to perpetuate his desire to better himself. Although these visits last only a few minutes, they are enough to keep him reminded of his discontent with his present life. Gradually, however, he becomes aware of Biddy. Her appearance has changed; she is now cleaner and fresher—not beautiful, but wholesome and sweet-tempered. She keeps pace with Pip in his studies, but she seems to learn everything he does without even trying. On a long Sunday walk on the marshes, Pip confides to her that he wants to become a gentleman because of Estella. Biddy (who secretly loves Pip) gives him the sensible advice that it's not worth changing his ways simply to spite Estella, and that if he has to change himself to win her, the girl is not worth winning.

Pip realizes that Biddy is a good woman and that Estella, at any given moment, might make him miserable. "If I could only get myself to fall in love with you—" he says to Biddy. "But you never will," she replies. On the way home, Joe's journeyman, Orlick, offers to walk along with them, and Biddy asks Pip to refuse, saying, "I am afraid he likes me." Pip does try to protect Biddy thereafter, but his thoughts roam. He is heavily discontent and is sustained only by the irrational hope that Miss Havisham will "make his fortune" when his apprenticeship is finished.

Commentary

Here we have, as it were, a framework for Pip's frustrations. Once, Joe's standards of living and his occupation were measurements of manhood for Pip. Now those standards have been scoffed at, ridiculed, and rejected by a girl whom Pip is infatuated with. Pip finds himself an "orphan" in a new world. He has no one to confide in, he has no mentor to guide him, and, most important, he has no money to realize his dreams of escaping what he has come to think of as "the common life." Estella is a cold siren, luring him, with the help of Miss Havisham, to another world.

Pip might have languished in his romantic imagination except for a single incident: some time ago, he helped an escaped convict. In Chapter 15, Dickens reintroduces the convict theme. The firing of guns at the Hulks announces that a prisoner has escaped, and a leg-iron is found next to Mrs. Joe, who has suffered a terrible blow on the back of her head.

Because of Mrs. Joe's "being silenced," Biddy comes to the household and soon begins to teach Pip to read and write, practical preparations for his future. The home life of Joe and Pip becomes more tranquil, but note that Pip is still dissatisfied by the day-in, day-out monotony of being a blacksmith's apprentice. Here, Dickens presents an especially suspenseful struggle between Pip's personal ambition and his discontent.

It is here, too, that Orlick, a sinister figure, is introduced into the story; during these chapters, hostility will increase between Pip and Orlick until Orlick will attempt to murder Pip.

CHAPTERS 18-19

Summary

One evening during the fourth year of Pip's apprenticeship, a group which includes Joe and Pip is gathered around the fire at the Jolly Bargemen listening to Mr. Wopsle read a newspaper account of a particularly vivid murder. Mr. Wopsle plays every role, and all agree to the verdict: willful murder.

He is interrupted by an authoritative stranger who proceeds to demonstrate Wopsle's complete ignorance of judicial procedure. After disposing of Wopsle, the stranger asks for Joe and Pip. Pip recognizes him as a burly gentleman he met once on the stairs at Miss Havisham's. When they arrive home to talk, the stranger announces that his name is Jaggers.

After determining that Joe will not hold Pip to his apprenticeship if there is something better in store for the lad, Jaggers tells Pip that he is "a young gentleman of great expectations." There are conditions, but they are simple: he must move from his present surroundings, and he must always bear the name of Pip. The name of his benefactor is to remain secret until it is revealed to him, and Pip is to make no inquiries whatever about this. A substantial sum of money has already been lodged with Jaggers, whom Pip is to regard as his guardian. Does Pip agree? Pip does. "My dream was out," he thinks. "Miss Havisham was going to make my fortune on a grand scale."

Jaggers suggests, first off, that Pip should take as his tutor Matthew Pocket, the same Matthew whom Pip had heard reviled at Satis House. Pip is then given twenty guineas to buy new clothes and is told to be in London in a week. When Jaggers again suggests that Joe accept the compensation he is authorized to pay, Joe becomes belligerent and Pip has to intervene. Money, Joe says, can never compensate "for the loss of the little child—what come to the forge—and ever the best of friends!"

Intoxicated with his good fortune, Pip nevertheless feels gloomy and lonely. Joe and Biddy are happy for him, but feel a great sadness about his leaving. Pip consents to show his new clothes to them after he buys them but to no one else in the village; that would be a "coarse and common business."

Pip strolls over the marshes in a farewell reverie and is joined by Joe before they return home. Later, with a condescension he supposes to be generosity, Pip tells Biddy that he proposes to improve Joe's manners and that he would like to raise him into a higher sphere. When Biddy replies that Joe is proud and might want to stay in a place he "fills well and with respect," Pip chides her as being envious and showing a "bad side of human nature." But at the tailoring establishment of Mr. Trabb and at the hatter's, the boot-maker's, and the hosier's, he finds the obsequiousness overwhelming but pleasant—exactly what he desires. At Pumblechook's, he is treated to an elaborate meal and greeted with much servility and handshaking.

On Friday, dressed in his new clothes, he visits Miss Havisham, who admits to having heard of his good fortune from Jaggers. On his last night at home, a fine dinner is served, but Pip, Biddy, and Joe all are "low, and none the higher for pretending to be in spirits."

Next morning at five, Pip leaves alone, unwilling to be seen in his new clothes alongside Joe, although he does not fully admit this. Once on the coach, he feels remorse and considers going back for a better parting. But he doesn't, for "the mists had all solemnly risen now," he recalls, "and the world lay spread before me."

Commentary

Chapters 18 and 19 bring to a close the first stage of Pip's "great expectations." Mr. Jaggers explains the mysterious circumstances of Pip's fortune and the stipulations necessary for Pip to acquire it. Pip is now free from his apprenticeship to Joe, but he is not quite free from his feelings of guilt. The goodness of Joe and Biddy, who are left behind, sustains the struggle in Pip's mind, even as his great expectations are at last about to be fulfilled.

Pip's expectations dazzle him. He does not yet realize how Miss Havisham has toyed with him; he believes her to be his "good angel," the answer to his prayers. Nor does he perceive the true worth of Biddy, who has taught him much and who has come to take care of him and Joe; now she is left behind him, a piece of his unpleasant past. Someday, however, she will become more prominent in Pip's life.

Pip is not completely happy, but happy or not, the orphan youth, with a new suit of clothes and money in his pocket, sets out for London, eager to become a gentleman worthy of the fair, if cold, Estella.

CHAPTERS 20-22

Summary

Arriving in London at last, Pip is terrified by the city's immensity; certainly it is not a fabled heaven on earth. In particular, the streets are "rather ugly, crooked, narrow, and dirty." Pip discovers, however, a pleasant surprise: Mr. Jaggers is a great man, despite the fact that his establishment in the unsavory district of Smithfield is unprepossessing, especially his dreary private office, dominated by two dreadful plaster casts of swollen faces. While waiting, Pip walks outside. The surroundings, including the slaughterhouse, the market around the corner, and Newgate Prison, he finds "sickening." But Mr. Jaggers, whom Pip encounters returning from his morning trials, is masterful. He is surrounded by hopeful clients, all of them obviously depending on Jaggers to save someone from jail or hanging. He deals with them in an arrogant and incisive fashion, characteristically shaking his huge forefinger at them and having to do only with those who have already paid their bills.

At the office, he settles Pip's business quickly while he wolfs down a sandwich and nips from a pocket flask of sherry. Pip is to go to Barnard's Inn to room with a young Mr. Pocket until Monday, when they will go to the elder Pocket's home, where Pip is to study. Pip also learns of his allowance, which is very liberal, and is given cards for tradesmen where his credit will be excellent. This is an advantage to Pip and also a means whereby Jaggers can check on his expenditures. Jaggers' clerk, Wemmick, walks with Pip to the inn.

Barnard's Inn proves to be a shockingly dingy collection of rotting buildings, where a notice on the letter-box announces that "Mr. Pocket, Jun." will return shortly. Pip is depressed. Pocket arrives, half an hour later, laden with fruit from Covent Garden Market, bought for Pip's arrival to supplement the food which, on Mr. Jaggers' instructions, Pip will supply. Pip is startled to find that he recognizes young Pocket. He is the "pale young gentleman" whom Pip skirmished with at Miss Havisham's.

Pip feels immediate rapport with his new friend, Herbert Pocket, who nicknames him Handel, after "The Harmonious Blacksmith," a piece of music by Handel. From Herbert, Pip learns Miss Havisham's story, sandwiched in between his first lessons about table manners.

Miss Havisham, the daughter of a wealthy brewer, was a spoilt child whose mother died when Miss Havisham was a baby. Later her father secretly married his cook, who bore him a son who turned out altogether bad. After first disinheriting him, the father relented on his deathbed and left him well off. The lad quickly squandered his inheritance and Miss Havisham was not inclined to help him. Then one day a new suitor appeared among her many callers and, to everyone's surprise, Miss Havisham fell passionately in love with him. He was not, Herbert's father had averred, a "gentleman," and he got great sums of money out of her, including the purchase of the half-brother's share of the brewery at a ridiculous price. Herbert's father, in fact, incurred her wrath by questioning her actions and has not seen her since.

On the day set for the wedding, the groom did not show up; instead, he wrote a letter which was received at twenty minutes to nine. It is supposed that the fiancé and the half-brother shared in the scheme, dividing the profits. Thenceforth, Miss Havisham devoted herself to seclusion and to bringing up Estella to wreak vengeance on the male sex. Of Estella's parents, Herbert knows nothing, only that Miss Havisham adopted her.

When Herbert begins to talk about his own prospects in the insurance business, Pip soon senses that, as in their fight, his hopes exceed his capabilities. This impression is reinforced when Pip discovers that the grimy counting-house, which he visits next day, pays Herbert absolutely nothing. Herbert is simply "in it" for the experience of looking about and learning about shipping, merchants, and insuring.

That evening, when they visit Pip's tutor, Herbert's father, Pip finds a somewhat addled Mr. Pocket reading under a tree with seven little Pockets "tumbling up" instead of growing up, under the casual supervision of two nurses, Flopson and Millers. Mr. Pocket understandably proves to be a "gentleman with a rather perplexed expression of face."

Commentary

Chapter 20 shows Pip's arrival in London and his first introduction to that city, the site of his next years of development. Throughout these chapters, Pip will be beginning a new life. Since he has left his friends and "family," these chapters will show him meeting new people who will influence the next portion of his life.

The first person he meets is Wemmick, Mr. Jaggers' clerk, who is responsible for looking after the financial aspects of Pip's career. Wemmick will turn out to be one of Dickens' most delightful creations with his enigmatic life style—his private Walworth life and emotions and, juxtaposed, his business life with its opposite emotions. Wemmick will later prove to be most helpful when Pip needs him. He is also categorized by the importance which he places on "portable property."

Mr. Jaggers' personality is also further developed. As in the scene with Pip and Joe, when Mr. Jaggers reveals that Pip has great expectations, Mr. Jaggers seems to conduct his business mainly by bullying people around. Dickens writes that "he seemed to bully his very sandwich as he ate it." And this was apparently the technique that he used to tame Molly, who will turn out to be Estella's mother.

As soon as Pip finds out that he is to share quarters with Herbert Pocket, and discovers that Herbert is the same young man whom he fought at Miss Havisham's, this fact serves to strengthen his belief that she is his benefactress. In this novel filled with coincidences, however, this is not necessarily one of them, since Mr. Jaggers, as we later find out, does not know any suitable young people other than Herbert Pocket, whom he knows only through Miss Havisham. Miss Havisham's story, as far as Herbert knows it, only verifies what Pip might have, and the reader probably has, suspected. The reasons for her doting attentions to Estella, her admonitions to "beggar" Pip and "break their hearts" (meaning men), are now clarified. Who Estella is and where she comes from remains a mystery. But for the first time Pip has had a look at Satis House through a friend's knowledgeable eyes.

Herbert is open and frank with Pip, qualities which will later influence Pip to set Herbert up in the business world. From Herbert, he hears all about Miss Havisham's past and is able to see that, unlike the other relatives of Miss Havisham, Herbert is not mean, impolite, or vindictive. At the end of Chapter 22, Herbert takes Pip out to the Pocket home, where he is exposed to the entire Pocket family, which is "tumbling up." Many scholars feel that the Pocket family is based on Dickens' own family since Dickens' wife apparently had no more talent for running a household than does Mrs. Pocket.

CHAPTERS 23-26

Summary

Mrs. Pocket, obsessed with the idea of social position, has "grown up highly ornamental, but perfectly helpless and useless," her sole occupation being reading books about the nobility. Matthew Pocket, who distinguished himself at Harrow and Cambridge, became a Grinder on acquiring Mrs. Pocket but, tiring of dull blades, he decided to come to London, where he supported himself on a modest income, on literary compilations and corrections, on tutoring, and by running a boarding house. Pip's fellow boarders (he decides to have a room here in addition to his quarters with Herbert) are Bentley Drummle, a dull young fellow who is "next heir but one to a baronetcy," and Startop, a younger and more attractive young man.

At dinner that night the confusions of the household are manifest. The servants run the house, the children run rampant, Mrs. Pocket is in her usual state of abstraction, and Mr. Pocket periodically tries to lift himself out of his chair by his own hair.

Mr. Pocket, who knows more of the plans for Pip's future than Pip does, proves surprisingly serious, honest, and practical as a tutor and advisor. Pip visits Jaggers to gain permission to maintain his establishment with Herbert at Barnard's Inn, and he again comes into contact with Wemmick, the head clerk. From Wemmick, Pip gets a further sense of the efficiency of Jaggers' professional manners; he learns, for example, that the two plaster casts in the inner office are replicas of two celebrated clients after they were hanged, and he discovers further that the jewelry which Wemmick wears came as gifts from clients who were also hanged. Wemmick values this curious jewelry as his "portable property."

Wemmick warns Pip that when he dines with Mr. Jaggers he will see "a wild beast tamed"—his housekeeper, whom Pip should keep his eye on. He also extends an invitation for Pip to visit him at home at Walworth. They end the day by watching Mr. Jaggers in action in police court. Pip's chief impression is that everybody is afraid of Jaggers: "Which side he was on, I couldn't make out, for he seemed to me to be grinding the whole place in a mill."

Eventually, Pip writes a note to Wemmick accepting an invitation for dinner. While they walk to Walworth together, Wemmick outlines dinner: stewed steak (home preparation) and cold fowl (which will be tender because the master of the cook-shop was once a juryman for whom Jaggers had done a favor); because the fowl came as a present, it is definitely considered "portable property." Wemmick also reveals to Pip that Jaggers *never* locks his house at night and boasts that he'd "want to see the man who'll rob *me.*"

Walworth is unusual. It resembles a castle, although it is the smallest house that Pip has ever seen, with imitation Gothic windows, a flagstaff, a moat four feet wide and two feet deep, a drawbridge, and a cannon which fires every night at nine o'clock

Greenwich time. In back are a pig, fowls, rabbits, and a small garden; in case of siege, Wemmick is prepared to hold out for a long time. Wemmick's father, the Aged Parent, is a clean, sprightly old man, very deaf, to whom his son is obviously devoted. They communicate by well-worn phrases and by nods, in which Pip actively participates. The main point of Wemmick's having the cannon is to give the Aged Parent something he can hear.

In the morning, as they return to the city, Wemmick retreats more and more into his hard, dry London self. When they arrive in their section, known as Little Britain, it is as if Wemmick's curious home and his Aged Parent had been "blown into space together."

One day Jaggers invites Pip, Herbert, Startop, and Drummle to dinner at his house in Soho, a stately but neglected house, of which he generally uses only the first floor. The lawyer takes a quick fancy to Drummle, whom he nicknames the Spider, and has him sit next to him. The dinner goes well, despite Drummle's temper and despite an episode in which Jaggers exposes a powerful scarred wrist of his housekeeper to prove that no man there is as strong as Molly. Pip later apologizes to Jaggers for Drummle's behavior, but Jaggers confides that he likes Drummle; he says that the fellow is "one of the true sort."

Commentary

In Chapter 23, we are introduced to two more young men who will influence Pip's life in one way or the other. Startop will later help him try to escape with Magwitch, and Drummle will later prove to be Pip's worst enemy and the source of great envy as Estella's husband.

Mrs. Pocket's pride in her ancestry should be contrasted with Pip's recent sense of pride and the pride which he will continue to develop until the end of the novel. Herbert apparently took after his father and not his mother. Also in contrast to Herbert are the other Pockets who come to visit Miss Havisham and who hate Pip with "the hatred of cupidity and disappointment."

Chapters 25 and 26 offer contrasting dinner parties. At Wemmick's house, everything is friendly and warm, if curious. Dickens takes great effort to make the reader see and appreciate the congenial relations between Wemmick and his father, often referred to as the "Aged P." Dickens is further developing the relationship between Pip and Wemmick so that Wemmick will be able to advise and help Pip later on.

In contrast to the warmth at Wemmick's house, we get an entirely different type of dinner at Mr. Jaggers' estate. His food is served by the mysterious Molly, whom Wemmick had earlier warned Pip about as being like a wild animal, tamed. Jaggers' exposing her wrist is his way of keeping her tame and keeping her under his control.

Jaggers' continued interest in the unpleasant Drummle must be accounted for as the latter's being a type that would attract the interest of an outstanding criminal lawyer. Note, here, that Jaggers warns Pip not to have much to do with the young man.

CHAPTERS 27-30

Summary

A letter from Biddy informs Pip that Joe is coming to town next day and will stop to see him at Barnard's Inn. Pip receives the news "with considerable disturbance, some mortification, and a keen sense of incongruity." In short, he is ashamed that someone might see the "common" blacksmith, especially Drummle, whom Pip despises.

Joe arrives, terribly self-conscious, and says that Mrs. Joe is no worse than before; Biddy is "ever right and ready"; all friends are the same except for Wopsle. He's "had a drop"—that is, he has left the church and has begun playacting on the stage. Joe sits down to tea and, to the accompaniment of many "Sirs," reveals that he has a message for Pip from Miss Havisham. Estella is home and would be glad to see him. On Biddy's advice, he has come to bring the message rather than having her write it. He readies himself to leave and refuses to return for dinner. "You and me is not two figures to be together in London," he says with simple dignity. When Pip can recover himself sufficiently, he goes out to look for Joe, but his old friend is gone.

Pip loses no time getting to see Estella; on the stagecoach next day, he finds himself in the company of two convicts who are being transported down to the Hulks. One of them, to his alarm, is the man who had used a file to stir his drink and had given Pip the two one-pound notes at the Jolly Bargemen; the convict, however, does not recognize Pip in his new gentleman's clothes. Waking from a doze, Pip hears the man talking about some money, and he learns that "his convict" had given the notes to this man with a request that he "find out that boy that had fed him and kep his secret." Pip gets out at the edge of town and goes to the Blue Boar, feeling that it would not be socially advisable for him to go to Joe's.

Convinced that Miss Havisham, who has adopted Estella and has "as good as adopted" him, intends for them to marry eventually, Pip goes to Satis House, where he is admitted by Orlick, now Miss Havisham's watchman. Pip finds Miss Havisham unchanged but Estella so grown-up and beautiful that at first he doesn't recognize her. As Pip and Estella walk together through the garden, she tells him that what was once fit company for him is not fit company now. He now feels certain that he should not visit Joe.

Back with Miss Havisham, Pip learns that Jaggers will come for dinner. Estella then leaves to dress, and Miss Havisham puts her arm around Pip's neck and says, "Love her, love her, love her." No matter how Estella hurts him, Pip is to love her. Jaggers enters, and Pip realizes that Miss Havisham, like everybody else, is afraid of him.

Jaggers and Pip talk, and Jaggers tells Pip that no one has seen Miss Havisham actually eat a meal since her dreadful wedding day. In answer to one of Pip's questions, Jaggers says that Estella's name is Havisham. After cards, Pip goes to bed and dreams of marrying her.

Next morning, Pip tells his guardian what he knows of Orlick's surly behavior as Miss Havisham's watchman, and Jaggers says that he will discharge the fellow from his post at once. Pip then takes a coach to London and there he immediately sends "a penitential codfish and barrel of oysters to Joe." He prepares to confide his feelings about Estella to Herbert, but it is not necessary; Herbert already knows and tries to dissuade him from his interest in the girl. The education she has had with Miss Havisham can lead only to trouble. Pip agrees but says he can't help it. Shortly thereafter, the two chaps discover a playbill Joe left announcing Mr. Wopsle's appearance in *Hamlet* that evening, and they set out to see the performance.

Commentary

Pip's false sense of pride and his ingratitude is brought to the forefront when he receives a letter from Biddy announcing the expected arrival of Joe for a visit. This news causes great consternation in Pip's mind and continues the conflict between the duty and love which he owes to Joe and his own "uncommon" personal ambitions. Pip admits that "if I could have kept him away by paying money, I certainly would have paid money." His fear is based on the anxiety caused by the possibility that Drummle, Pip's worst enemy, might catch a glimpse of the rustic Joe and therefore make Pip an object of ridicule. Thus, Pip realizes, "our worst weaknesses and meannesses are usually committed for the sake of the people whom we most despise."

In contrast to Pip's false pride is the simple dignity of Joe. Pip is so tense about Joe's visit that he makes Joe tense also. When they are alone, Joe is able to explain in simple language that carries with it a ring of true dignity the nature of their relationship—that if Pip ever wants to see him, he won't look nearly so foolish in his work clothes at the forge as he does in his suit here in London. Pip fails to recognize that Joe also has a sense of pride, and not false pride, in his own work.

The thought of Estella intensifies Pip's shame of his origin, and he cannot conceive of staying at Joe's and also visiting Estella; thus, he hypocritically deceives himself that it would be inconvenient for him to stay at Joe's. Along with the revival of the Estella theme is the re-emergence of the convict theme. The convict whom Pip had seen stirring his drink with the file is also on the carriage which carries Pip to meet Estella; Dickens is constantly reminding us of the interchange of these two ideas.

When Pip again sees Estella, he hardly recognizes the elegant and beautiful lady as being the same Estella whom he once played cards with. And whereas earlier, fear of Drummle prevented Pip from receiving Joe openly, now the elegance of Estella puts all notions of visiting Joe out of the question. The only connection between Joe's forge and Miss Havisham's Satis House is Orlick, Pip's evil nemesis; since he works as the gatekeeper there, Pip's part in getting Orlick fired will later be part of the reason that Orlick tries to murder Pip.

On his return to London, Pip confesses his love for Estella to Herbert and discovers that in addition to his being warned by Estella herself, Herbert also thinks that Estella is incapable of love. Thus we perceive that Dickens is building a contrast between three love affairs: Herbert confesses his love and intent to marry Clara, and we have heard of Wemmick's and Miss Skiffins's love for each other; only the last of the trio, Pip's love for Estella, is destined for sadness.

CHAPTERS 31-33

Summary

To call the production of *Hamlet*, in which Mr Wopsle stars, amateurish would be an unwarranted compliment. Nevertheless, despite the shabby character of the whole production and the jeers and jests from the audience which Pip and Herbert have to laugh at in spite of themselves, Pip "had a latent impression that there was something decidedly fine in Mr. Wopsle's elocution." After the performance, an emissary from Mr. Waldengarver (Wopsle's stage name) intercepts them and invites them to visit Wopsle backstage. The conversation between them and this messenger, who is the owner of the costumes which Pip and Herbert have been laughing at, consists entirely of how well Wopsle showed off the costumes.

A letter from Estella, with neither salutation nor regards, informs Pip that he is to meet her on the midday coach. Pip arrives at the coach-office almost five hours early, where he has the good fortune to encounter Wemmick, who invites him to visit Newgate prison with him. The experience is most unpleasant; Pip finds the prison a "frouzy, ugly, disorderly, depressing scene." Wemmick, however, walks "among the prisoners much as a gardener might walk among his plants." He is, Pip realizes, both highly popular and respected. At one point, Wemmick introduces Pip to a "Colonel," a counterfeiter who is shortly to be hanged; the evidence was too strong, and Jaggers has lost the case. The Colonel regrets he cannot afford a good ring to give Wemmick, but the latter suggests a brace of pigeons, certainly "portable property," as it were.

After a three-hour wait, during which Pip meditates on the role which prison and crime have played in his life, he suddenly sees Estella's beautiful face and her hand waving to him from a coach. She gives Pip a purse to pay the expenses for a carriage to Richmond, where she is to live, then for the second time, she lets Pip kiss her cheek, commenting all the time about their fates "being disposed of by others." The person with whom she will be staying, she says, is a well-placed lady who can introduce her to the right people, and Pip, she adds, has been given the freedom to visit her freely.

Commentary

These chapters do little or nothing to move the plot forward. Chapter 31, dealing with Mr. Wopsle (or Mr. Waldengarver, as he is known on the stage), is both a hilariously funny and, at the same time, a pathetic story of his bumbling failure.

Chapter 32 is a digression, the type of which is quite famous in the Dickens canon of writing. The digression was intended to call attention to the disgraceful conditions in London prisons. Dickens, who was very concerned with penal reforms, uses any available opportunity to draw attention to them. However, as an artist, Dickens also includes an implied contrast between the low and sordid conditions in the prison and the beauty, pride, and elegance of Estella; and there is also the later knowledge that Estella's origins are closely connected with Newgate prison, and that Pip's great expectations are also connected with prison life. Thus there is a certain irony connected with Pip's desire to protect Estella even from the knowledge of Newgate, thinking her too superior even to hear about this horrible place.

When Estella first arrives, and every time he meets her during this stage of his life, he is strangely haunted by some familiarity to someone else whom he has recently seen. It will be much later, however, before he is able to make the connection between Estella and Molly.

The only plot development in this section is that Estella, in being placed with Mrs. Brandley, will now be moving out into society, will meet the odious Drummle, and will cause Pip even more distress.

CHAPTERS 34-35

Summary

Pip's guilt about how he feels toward Joe and Biddy continues to bother him, but he remains bound to Estella, and contributing to his discomfort is the fact that he has fallen into debt and has led Herbert, who has no financial expectations, along with him.

One evening as Pip and Herbert are trying to organize their finances, a black-bordered letter arrives for Pip. It is from Trabb & Company, informing him that his sister has died and that his presence is requested at the funeral the following Monday.

Pip is troubled all week long by memories, somewhat softened by time, of a sister whom he has no reason to remember fondly. Later, he walks along the familiar streets of his childhood, still feeling the loss until he finds that Joe's house has been taken over temporarily by Mr. Trabb, the tailor, who doubles as undertaker. The mourners, of whom Joe is chief, are dressed stiffly in black, and Pumblechook, busy with sherry and food, is as obsequious as ever.

After the burial, Pip walks with Biddy awhile. Biddy is moving to Mrs. Hubble's and is hopeful of becoming a teacher in a newly finished school. Mrs. Joe died quietly, she says, her head on Joe's shoulder, saying "Joe," "Pardon," and, finally, "Pip." Orlick, now apparently working in the quarries, still seems to be shadowing her. Pip tells her he will often come down to see Joe, and he reproaches her angrily when she indicates doubts and insists on calling him "Mr. Pip." That night, he is restless and has trouble sleeping. He broods about Biddy's lack of faith in his character. Next morning, he leaves, promising to come back, but with an inner knowledge that Biddy is right; he probably will not.

Commentary

Chapter 34 shows Pip becoming accustomed to someday receiving "great expectations" and, as a result, he begins to go deeper and deeper in debt. He is beginning to squander his money, a perilous course, especially later when his expectations no longer exist. Then he will be in dire circumstances and will be faced with the dilemma of accepting money either from Magwitch, the convict, or from Miss Havisham, neither of whom is obligated to him.

Chapter 35, which presents the details of the funeral, gives a vivid picture of the social customs of the time connected with burial rites. Pip is troubled because he can feel so little sorrow over his sister's death. Even though his memories of Mrs. Joe are softened by her death, there was never any deep love between them, nothing to compare with the feelings between himself and Joe; consequently, true remorse is replaced by simple regret.

Still, however, Pip is very defensive about his relationship with Joe. His sense of superiority keeps him at a distance from both Joe and Biddy, and as he talks with Biddy about his intent to leave London and visit them more often, Biddy's remarks indicate her knowledge that Pip will probably not visit them. Pip knows that Biddy is correct, and we know that Pip will have to undergo a significant change before he recognizes the true worth of both Biddy and Joe.

CHAPTERS 36-39

Summary

On the day of Pip's "majority"—that is, his twenty-first birthday—he calls by invitation at Mr. Jaggers' office. There he receives congratulations, a banknote for five hundred pounds, and the information that this amount will hereafter be his yearly allowance, drawn quarterly, until his benefactor chooses to reveal himself. He is now in charge of his own financial affairs. At work, and feeling generous, he makes tentative inquiries to Wemmick about ways to help Herbert in his business career and discovers that this is a question which will have to be asked later to the "Walworth Wemmick" (the "private" self that lives in the curious castle cottage).

Arriving at Wemmick's castle, Pip finds the Union Jack flag flying and the drawbridge up. The Aged P. admits him quite peacefully and futilely attempts conversation until a sign pops out beside the fireplace chimney which says "John." Wemmick is home, and the Aged P., trailed by Pip, hurries out to lower the drawbridge and admit him. Wemmick is accompanied by Miss Skiffins, an angular maiden whose dress makes her look like a boy's kite. That she is a regular visitor is soon evidenced by another demonstration of the chimney signs, this one reading "Miss Skiffins."

While tea is being prepared, Pip tells Wemmick about his desire to anonymously help Herbert buy into a small partnership. Wemmick thinks this is a fine idea and says that he will help Pip. Before the week is out, he hears from Wemmick that a Mr. Skiffins, the angular lady's accountant-brother, has found a fine possibility. After much consultation, matters are arranged for Herbert to be employed by a young shipping-broker, keeping Pip's involvement secret. Herbert's joy over his unexpected "opening" at Clarriker's (the broker's) brings Pip his first feeling that his expectations have at last done some good.

After Pip's interminable visits to the house in Richmond where Estella is staying (during which he has not enjoyed "one hour's happiness in her society; and yet my mind all round the four-and-twenty hours was harping on the happiness of having her with me unto death"), he learns one day that he is to take Estella on a visit to Satis House. Miss Havisham's obsession with Estella's conquests, including Pip, is more intense than ever. Though he sees clearly that "Estella was set to wreak Miss Havisham's revenge" on him, he still believes that eventually she will be assigned to him permanently.

During the visit there, Pip hears the first sharp words that he has ever heard between Miss Havisham and Estella. The old lady accuses Estella of growing tired of her and pleads for love. Estella, perfectly composed, replies that she is only behaving as cold and hard as Miss Havisham trained her to be. Pip is given a place to sleep in Satis House for the first time. He sees and hears Miss Havisham walking about, ghostly and agitated.

Back in London, Pip dines at a fancy gentleman's club, and he and Drummle nearly come to blows after Drummle proposes a toast to a lady friend, Estella. Later observations at Richmond prove to Pip that Estella is deliberately encouraging Drummle's romantic attention. Pip protests, but Estella tells him candidly that she deceives and entraps everyone but Pip. Pip is unable to understand.

Pip becomes twenty-three, and one day as he is reading a book in the new quarters he shares with Herbert, he hears a footstep on the stair below. It is a muscular stranger about sixty years old, gray haired, browned by the sun, and roughly dressed. Once inside the apartment, he gazes around with obvious pleasure and holds out both hands to Pip. Pip recoils, not recognizing the man until the stranger abruptly takes out a file, wraps a handkerchief around his head, and hugs himself and shivers. Pip knows him: it's his convict.

The man tells him that Pip was generous to him on the marshes and he has never forgotten it. Pip holds him off, then thanks him loftily, pointing out that under his new circumstances he cannot be expected to renew a chance acquaintance of long ago. Yet the man stays for tea and explains that he has been living as a sheep farmer in New South Wales, Australia, and has done wonderfully well. When Pip condescendingly repays the two one-pound notes, the man burns them. Gradually, by revealing an intimate knowledge of the way Pip's money has come to him, the old stranger lets Pip realize that it was *he*, not Miss Havisham, who has been his bene-factor. "Yes, Pip, dear boy," he says, "I've made a gentleman on you! It's me wot has done it!"

Overwhelmed by repugnance and disappointment, Pip asks desperately if there was no one else but the old convict involved. The answer is negative. Only the knowledge that the old man was mak-ing Pip a finer gentleman than any of the colonists who looked down at him has enabled him to bear up through a hard struggle.

Afterward, Pip sits dejected by the fire, his dreams about Miss Havisham and Estella shattered, his guilt about Joe intensified, and his worry about the convict's safety intensified by his fear and his dislike of him.

Commentary

Pip's basic nature is generous, as we see in Chapter 36, when he begins to receive the first of his "great expectations." He immedi-ately wishes to help Herbert Pocket get started in business and his first action is with that in mind. But we should also remember that Pip's love for Estella has made him blind to the simple dignity of Joe and Biddy; only when he learns the full truth of Estella's parent-age and the source of his own "great expectations" will he recognize the true worth of his old friends.

In contrast to Mr. Jaggers, who is always the same whether in business or at dinner, Wemmick gives Pip one opinion about in-vesting "portable property" at the business office and will give another and completely different one when Pip calls upon him at Walworth. Thus, Chapter 37 continues to show Pip's basic gener-osity as the secret plot to help Herbert is initiated. Also, at Wal-worth, Wemmick is comically involved in his love skirmishes with Miss Skiffins—a contrast to the relationship between Pip and Estella.

In Chapter 38, the scene between Miss Havisham and Estella should have made it perfectly clear to Pip that Estella is incapable of any emotion or true feelings: her heart is made of stone. Actually

Pip does recognize part of this truth, but his love for Estella blinds him to the full truth: "I saw in this, that Estella was set to wreak Miss Havisham's revenge on men, and that she was not to be given to me until she had gratified it." This chapter also contains the beginning of the relationship between Estella and Drummle, Pip's worst enemy. Why Estella attaches herself to Drummle is a mystery to many people. Most critics suggest that Dickens had the end of the novel in mind and knew that Estella must be subdued and must suffer, and that it would take such a brute as Drummle to effect this change in Estella. In fact, Estella's most honest statement is that she does not lay any traps for Pip, and that she is honest and open only with Pip.

In Chapter 39, the first major crisis of the novel occurs with the revelation that Pip's benefactor is the convict whom he helped when he was a young lad. That all of his great expectations relied upon a convict, an unmentionable in society, and not from Miss Havisham, is the most dramatic situation that Pip has had to face. But, finally, many truths are clear to him. He now knows that he has been used by Miss Havisham as "a convenience, a sting for the greedy relations." He also realizes that Estella was never meant for him, and his connections with a convict further remove her from his world. And, in addition, he realizes with great remorse that he deserted Joe for this convict.

It is fortunate that Magwitch, the convict, is so completely engrossed in seeing Pip again as a gentleman that he is totally oblivious to the horror he creates in Pip. "The abhorrence in which I held the man, the dread I had of him, the repugnance with which I shrank from him, could not have been exceeded if he had been some terrible beast." Yet it is to Pip's credit that he has absolutely no thought of betraying this man and immediately accepts the burden of protecting the returned convict who, if caught, will be hanged. That the convict so loves Pip as to risk his own life in order to see him is an additional burden upon Pip. Thus ends the second stage of Pip's expectations.

CHAPTERS 40-42

Summary

When Abel Magwitch, as the convict reveals his name to be, awakens, Pip tells him about a mysterious man whom he saw crouched on the stairs. The stranger eluded him, however; Magwitch hopes that he is not known in London and that he was not followed. He faces certain death if he is caught, and since he was last tried here in London, the possibility of his being recognized certainly does exist. Pip then suggests that Magwitch pass as his "uncle," using his shipboard name of Provis. "Provis" agrees and gives Pip a thick pocketbook, railing against "every one, from the judge in his wig, to the colonist a-stirring up the dust." Pip, he says, is a better gentleman than all of them put together.

When Pip talks with Jaggers, the lawyer confirms that Magwitch is indeed Pip's sole benefactor. Pip's dreams about Miss Havisham's generosity have no foundation. Pip returns and tries to outfit the convict in new clothes with no luck: "Prisoner, Felon, and Bondsman" are written all over him. Herbert arrives, wins Magwitch's approval, and is sworn to secrecy on a greasy little black Testament.

After Magwitch is moved to safe quarters nearby, Pip and Herbert try to decide on a plan of action. Herbert understands Pip's repugnance for the convict and his reluctance to take any more money. Perhaps, he suggests, they should find out more about Magwitch.

Agreeing to tell the lads more about himself, Magwitch begins by saying that he has no idea where he was born or who his parents were. He has been in jail and out of jail over and over; a deserting soldier taught him to read and a "travelling Giant" taught him to write. He finally made connections with a man named Compeyson, who considered himself a bit of a gentleman and hired Magwitch to do his dirty work for him. Compeyson, who had "no more heart than an iron file," kept him busy "swindling, handwriting forging, stolen bank-note passing, and such-like." Slowly, Compeyson involved Magwitch deeper and deeper in his schemes, but Magwitch insists that he was careful never to involve his own wife—of whom we hear no more for the present.

Eventually Compeyson and Magwitch were tried together on a felony charge. Compeyson, however, looking like a perfect gentleman, was recommended for mercy. Compeyson was sentenced to seven years, Magwitch to fourteen. Magwitch swore then that someday he would smash in Compeyson's face, and at last, when he escaped the prison ship and Compeyson followed by the same route, he had his opportunity. Compeyson, Pip realizes, was the *second* convict on the marshes. For escaping, Compeyson was punished lightly but Magwitch was sentenced for life.

While Magwitch explains that he doesn't know whether Compeyson is dead, Herbert hands Pip a note scribbled on the cover of a book: "Young Havisham's name was Arthur. Compeyson is the man who professed to be Miss Havisham's lover."

Commentary

Pip is deeply troubled as to how to protect his "dreaded visitor." Immediately, suspicion is aroused when the door keeper confirms that another person came immediately after Magwitch arrived. Later we learn that Magwitch's every move has been observed since he left New South Wales.

What might have seemed to be too many coincidences at first are somewhat reduced by the fact that Magwitch once used Jaggers as his lawyer. Furthermore, the fact that Jaggers is one of the most famous lawyers of London would partly account for the coincidence that both Miss Havisham and Magwitch used him. However, since the requests of both Miss Havisham and Magwitch are idiosyncratic, it is understandable that both would seek the aid of one of London's most renowned lawyers, and one who is well versed in all types of activities.

When Pip goes to Jaggers for verification of who his benefactor really is, he is still hoping, albeit rather feebly, that Magwitch is *not* the one. Using very careful language so as not to implicate himself, Jaggers is able to confirm that Magwitch of New South Wales is indeed Pip's sole benefactor, and he convinces Pip that he has never given any indication that it was Miss Havisham. Everything was circumstantial evidence, not to be relied upon in a court of law.

In Chapter 42, however, coincidence might test the reader's credulity. As Magwitch tells about his past, the fact that he was once a partner with the man who betrayed Miss Havisham and that both Magwitch and Miss Havisham have been the victims of Compeyson will tend to test one's credulity. However, Magwitch's story creates suspense when the convict refers to a wife with whom he once had some trouble. This clue becomes more important later in tracing Estella's parentage. Further suspense is created by the rumor that Compeyson, Magwitch's enemy, is probably still at large in England and possibly in London.

CHAPTERS 43-44

Summary

Pip speculates on how much of "his shrinking from Provis might be traced to Estella," and to "the abyss between Estella in her pride and beauty, and the returned transport whom [he has] harbored," and decides to see Estella and Miss Havisham one last time before he leaves the country with Provis. Finding that Estella has gone to Satis House alone, Pip goes after her. Arriving at the Blue

Boar by coach, he finds Drummle at the inn; he is down visiting Estella and will dine with her that evening. Pip and Drummle indulge in a bit of childish arguing and pushing one another, then Drummle rides off, and Pip sets out for Satis House.

Miss Havisham seems taken aback at Pip's arrival; why has he come? Pip explains that he has found out at last who his patron is. Miss Havisham admits that she furthered his delusion that she was his benefactress, and asks, "Who am I, for God's sake, that I should be kind?" She states, "You made your own snares. *I* never made them." Pip asks nothing for himself but does ask that she continue the help he has begun for Herbert, which he can no longer continue for reasons which are somebody else's secret, not his. He then turns to Estella and tells her that he has always loved her; to his amazement, he learns that she is soon to be married to Drummle. He pleads eloquently that she "not let Miss Havisham lead you into this fatal step." Estella, calm as usual, explains that it is entirely her idea. Miss Havisham wants her to wait, but she is bored with the life she is leading.

Downhearted, Pip arrives at the porter's gate at his lodgings in London and is given a note in Wemmick's handwriting, which he reads by the porter's lantern: "Don't Go Home."

Commentary

In these chapters, Pip is trying to salvage what he can from his life. He is sorely disappointed that his benefactor for these many years has been a common convict, yet his pride is still with him, even though he recognizes the "abyss between Estella in her pride and beauty" and himself. This same pride earlier made him spurn Joe. But now he uses Joe as an excuse to go back to Miss Havisham's for a final farewell and to confront her with this new knowledge.

In this troubled state of mind, he is even more annoyed to discover that his only enemy (Drummle) is also staying at the inn. The scene between the two is amusing, but not very significant to the novel, except to make it more difficult for Pip to realize that his beloved Estella is giving herself to the scoundrel.

In his interview with Miss Havisham, it is to Pip's credit that he shows no rancor and no hatred after he realizes that he has been used by her. He is calm enough to confront his failing fortunes and try to get help so that Herbert's place in the Clarriker firm will be assured. Again, Pip's generous and thoughtful nature is emphasized as he makes a last effort to benefit a friend.

Pip's confession of the depth of his love for Estella has no effect on the young woman, who has continually warned Pip that she has no feelings. Surprisingly, however, Miss Havisham apparently feels the effect of Pip's deep, genuine words of adoration for Estella and begins to have remorse over her actions, thereby initiating a reversal in her character.

CHAPTERS 45-48

Summary

After spending a night hiding in a miserable inn, Pip hurries early next morning to Walworth, where Wemmick greets him cheerfully and tells him that he has learned that a certain person of not "uncolonial pursuits, and not unpossessed of portable property" has caused a stir by disappearing from his part of the world and that Pip's chambers in Garden Court are being watched. Pip also learns that Compeyson is living in London, and he deduces that Compeyson is involved.

Wemmick, meanwhile, has consulted Herbert and has advised him that Provis should be moved at once to the upper floor of the house in which Herbert's fiancée lives with her invalid father. The place is on the river so that it will be easy to get Provis aboard a ship when the time is ripe and Pip will be able to get regular news of his benefactor through Herbert. Time being short, Provis is already installed; Pip can visit him tonight before going home, but then must stay away. No attempt to get Provis out of the country should be made until things have quieted.

After a peaceful day with the Aged P., Pip sets out for Provis' new quarters. He has difficulty, however, finding Mill Pond Bank, which he knows only to be at Chink's Basin on the river, by the Old Green Copper Rope-Walk, in an area of ship repair yards. Finding the house at last, he is introduced to Herbert's fiancée, Clara, a charming dark-eyed girl of about twenty, obviously devoted to Herbert.

Provis, now lodged as "Campbell," is comfortably settled in two fresh and airy rooms. Pip finds him inexplicably softened. Omitting mention of Compeyson, he tells him what Wemmick has told him. Provis is agreeable to everything, including Pip's not changing his way of living at present, despite the funds in the thick pocketbook. Herbert suggests that Pip get a boat, which they can anchor at Temple stairs. Both of them being good oarsmen, they can make daily trips up and down the river until people are accustomed to seeing them. At the right time, they can take Provis to a ship themselves. Provis approves the scheme. Next day, Pip buys the boat and rowing begins.

Pip, having sent the unopened pocketbook back to Magwitch, has had to begin selling his jewelry. He broods over his last meeting with Estella, but his main worry is the possibility of Magwitch's capture. Weeks of inaction fret him.

One evening, after having rowed downriver and having seen the signal that all is well (a lowered blind), Pip is intercepted by Jaggers, who invites him to dinner, saying Wemmick will also be there. Wemmick, who is as dry and distant to Pip "as if there were twin Wemmicks and this was the wrong one," has a message from Miss Havisham. Pip is to come down on the "little matter of business" he had mentioned to her. Pip does so, and when Molly, the house-keeper, enters the room, Pip suddenly realizes who the nameless shadow is that has been haunting him. Molly's "hands were Estella's hands and her eyes were Estella's eyes." This woman is Estella's mother! As Pip and Wemmick leave, Pip asks about Molly's past history, and Wemmick tells him what he knows. Molly's case was the one which made Jaggers' reputation. It was a desperate case. She was accused of strangling to death an older and much bigger woman out of jealousy over a "tramping man." Jaggers demonstrated that the scratches on Molly's hands could have been caused by brambles, some of which were found embedded there. There was also talk that Molly had killed her own daughter as revenge against this same man, but Jaggers showed that this was not an issue in the trial. The jury gave in, and immediately after her acquittal, Molly went into Jaggers' service, where she has remained ever since.

Commentary

Essentially, these chapters begin to unravel the many complications that have been set up and therefore move the plot on towards its end. Having received the note from Wemmick, Pip goes the next day, and suspense is heightened by the knowledge that Compeyson is indeed in London.

Wemmick also strongly advises Pip to hang onto any "portable property." Both Wemmick and Pip know that if Magwitch is caught, *all* of his property goes to the state. Therefore, in Chapter 47, when Pip returns the money without touching a bit of it even though he is being hounded by creditors, even Pip cannot say whether he did it out of a true or false satisfaction or motive.

While dining at Jaggers', Pip is more convinced than ever that Molly, Jaggers' maid, is really Estella's mother, and upon further inquiry through Wemmick, he is now convinced that this is the truth.

CHAPTERS 49-51

Summary

Pip finds Miss Havisham brooding before the fire in a room across from her own. Although she fears that Pip "can never believe, now, that there is anything human" in her heart, she wishes to show him that she is not made of stone and that she genuinely wants to help Herbert. With difficulty, because her attention wanders, Pip explains the situation in detail. Nine hundred pounds is needed to complete the purchase of Herbert's partnership. After inquiring about Pip's happiness and desiring to help him too, she tells him that it is noble of him to say that he has causes of unhappiness that she knows nothing about; she then gives him a note to take to Jaggers for the money. Handing him the tablets on which she has written, she says, "My name is on the first leaf. If you can ever write under my name, 'I forgive her,' though ever so long after my broken heart is dust—pray do it!"

She then becomes emotional and tells Pip that for years she hoped to save Estella from her own fate, but finally she realizes that she "stole her [Estella's] heart away and put ice in its place." She doesn't know whose child Estella really is. Long ago she asked Jaggers to bring her a little girl to rear and love, and one night he brought the child she called Estella. Of this, Estella knows nothing, and Miss Havisham learned nothing more about Estella.

After parting from Miss Havisham, Pip walks around the place. Disturbed, he stops back to check on her and finds her ablaze; sitting too close to the fire, she ignited her flowing garments. Pip rolls on the floor with her, smothering the flames with his cloak and burning himself severely in the process. When the doctor arrives, he says that she is seriously burned, but that the real danger is nervous shock. She is treated on the table where her cobwebbed wedding cake has rested, the place where she had long before sworn she would be laid out in death one day. During the night she regularly repeats, "What have I done!" and "Take a pencil and write under my name, 'I forgive her,' " a sentence she continues to repeat as Pip kisses her goodbye before taking the early morning coach.

Herbert, who tends to Pip's burns, tells him that Provis has confided in him about the "missis" he spoke of (Chapter 42). She was tried for strangling another woman, a larger and older woman, and her acquittal was won by Jaggers. After the murder she swore to Magwitch that she would destroy her child and vanish until she was caught and tried. Provis believes that she carried out her threat. Compeyson knew the story and used it as a means of keeping his power over Magwitch. This is what "barbed the point of Provis' animosity" toward Compeyson. The girl would now be about Pip's age; Pip's appearance on the marshes when he was seven reminded the convict of his own little lost daughter. As Herbert tells the story, Pip realizes that the man they have in hiding down the river is Estella's father.

Next morning, Pip gives Jaggers the details of Miss Havisham's accident, and he reveals that Miss Havisham has told him all she knows about Estella. But Pip himself knows more about the mystery. He knows who Estella's mother and father are. Jaggers clearly does not know about the father, and he is, for the first time, genuinely startled when Pip says that it is "Provis—from New South Wales." When Jaggers, after Pip's full explanation, drops the subject and proposes to return to work, Pip makes a passionate appeal for more information. Jaggers then reveals that he took the baby to Miss Havisham because this is one child from the many he had seen growing up in a life of crime and poverty that he could save. It had been a secret until Pip got wind of it, and no one, he convinces Pip, particularly Estella, will be helped if the secret goes further. Jaggers and Wemmick then resume work on rather ill terms, which are alleviated only when they combine to throw out a perennially snivelling client.

Commentary

These chapters deal with the continued unraveling of the mystery surrounding Estella's parentage. Pip, for example, receives new information when he goes to visit Miss Havisham. When he first sees her, he is surprised by the tremendous change. She is no longer hard and cynical. Seeing Pip suffer so greatly has renewed all her own suffering and has caused her to realize all the suffering she has caused Pip. As an expression of her regret, she will fulfill Pip's request that Herbert Pocket be helped. Again, even though Pip is deeply in debt, he refuses any financial help from Miss Havisham for himself, and he freely forgives her for everything that she has done to him. Thus, in spite of the manner in which he has treated poor old Joe, Pip is rapidly rising in the estimation of the reader.

During the fire, Pip's attempt to rescue Miss Havisham causes serious burns, which will severely handicap his usefulness in helping

Magwitch to escape. Again, it is to Pip's credit that he takes great personal risks in order to save Miss Havisham. It is furthermore ironic that she is so severely burned because everything is so rotten with age that it crumbled and shredded in Pip's grasp.

With information gathered from Miss Havisham, then from Herbert's narration of Magwitch's wife and child, Pip is able to conclude the parentage of Estella and is able to confront, and for once confound, Jaggers with his discoveries. The only use he will ever make of the information is to delight Magwitch with it on Magwitch's death bed.

CHAPTERS 52-53

Summary

One Monday at breakfast, Pip receives the following letter from Wemmick: "Walworth. Burn this as soon as read. Early in the week, or say Wednesday, you might do what you know of, if you felt disposed to try it. Now burn." Pip and Herbert resolve to do it, and because Pip's arms were disabled by the burns, they take a friend of Pip's to row in place of him. They then study the schedules of all outbound ships in preparation for placing Magwitch aboard one. Pip also plans to go with his benefactor.

Then another note is placed in Pip's box: "If you are not afraid to come to the old marshes to-night or to-morrow night at nine, and to come to the little sluice-house by the limekiln, you had better come. If you want information regarding your Uncle Provis, you had much better come and tell no one and lose no time. You must come alone. Bring this with you." Bewildered, Pip takes the next coach down. Awaiting nighttime, he visits Satis House and is informed that Miss Havisham is "still very ill, though considered something better."

When Pip reaches the sluice-house, there is no answer to his knock. The door is open, so he enters, but he finds himself suddenly trapped by a noose thrown over him from behind and tied securely to a wall. When his assailant lights a candle, Pip sees that it is Orlick, who says that he lured Pip here to kill him. Pip cost him his job as a guard at Miss Havisham's and came between him and Biddy. Orlick means to kill him and then burn his body in the limekiln. Pip, his mind working "with inconceivable rapidity," fears the terrible death ahead of him, but dreads even more the fact that everyone will think that he deserted them, and that he will be "misremembered after death." Orlick, drinking steadily to get his courage up, tells Pip that he now works for Compeyson and that it was he who was hiding on the stairs the night of Magwitch's arrival.

As Orlick comes toward Pip with a stone-hammer in his hand, Pip gives a great shout, and figures burst in as Orlick, emerging "from a struggle of men," runs out into the night. Pip, who faints, revives to find Herbert beside him.

Since there is no time to pursue Orlick, they hurry back to London, treating Pip's painful arm all the way. After a half delirious day and night in bed, Pip wakens early to begin their great adventure.

Commentary

Pip's generosity is finally attested to as he completes the arrangements to have Herbert set up in business, at least as far as he can go at the present moment. To his credit also is his sincere desire to help the man who has been his benefactor. Consequently, Pip feels that it is necessary to check upon the mysterious letter that he receives. His loyalty emerges as a welcome and positive attribute.

On his way to the meeting place, in the marsh country, Pip seems to realize how unfair he has been to Joe and Biddy and he seems to be truly repentant. This might be termed as one of the turning points in his moral regeneration.

We should remember in this section that Orlick has been Pip's evil nemesis since childhood, and the scene, while having little to do at this time with the main plot, allows the reader to know that it definitely was Orlick who gave Mrs. Joe her fatal injury. Other than hearing that he was jailed later for breaking into Mr. Pumblechook's house, we hear no more of Orlick.

CHAPTERS 54-56

Summary

The young men start downriver at nine, when the tide changes. Pip carries a bag filled with "the few necessaries" he will need, come what may. After picking up Magwitch at Mill Pond stairs on schedule and finishing a hard row against the tide, they reach an inn that evening. It is a dirty place, but no one else is in the house.

During the night, Pip is awakened by a noise and sees two men peering into their boat. Next morning, they sight a steamer and are preparing to board it when a four-oared galley shoots out from the bank a little ways beyond them. As the two boats come alongside each other, the galley's steersman calls on them to surrender

Magwitch and drives his boat into theirs. He seizes Magwitch, and Magwitch pulls the cloak from the sitter beside the steersmen, revealing Compeyson. Pip's boat overturns right in the steamer's path. Taken aboard the galley, Pip finds Herbert and their friend, Startop, there; the two convicts are missing. Magwitch soon appears, swimming, and is taken aboard and manacled; he has a severe chest injury and a deep cut in his head. There is no sign of Compeyson.

Back at the inn, Pip gets permission to buy new clothes for Magwitch (whose possessions, including the pocket-book, are confiscated) and to accompany him back to London. "Now," Pip tells us, "my repugnance to him had all melted away, and in the hunted, wounded, shackled creature who held my hand in his, I only saw a man who had meant to be my benefactor, and who had felt affectionately, gratefully, and generously towards me with great constancy through a series of years. I only saw in him a much better man than I had been to Joe."

Magwitch is content to take his chances. "I've seen my boy," he says, "and he can be a gentleman without me." Pip, realizing that all Magwitch's possessions will be confiscated, also understands that Magwitch need never know this.

Despite Jaggers' aid in a hopeless case, Magwitch is indicted. But he remains in ignorance of the fact that Pip will not inherit his property.

Next Monday, Pip meets Wemmick for a morning walk. Wemmick is carrying a fishing rod and says he just likes to walk with it. In quick succession, Wemmick finds a church which he suggests they enter; white gloves in his pocket, which he suggests they put on; Miss Skiffins, whom he suggests marrying; the Aged P., who needs help to get his gloves on; a clergyman; and a ring. The Aged P., despite not hearing the clergyman, manages to give the bride away, and the party repairs to a nearby tavern for an excellent breakfast. "Now, Mr. Pip," Wemmick says, shouldering his fishing-rod, "let me ask you whether anybody would suppose this to be a wedding party!"

Pip regularly visits Magwitch in the prison infirmary. The convict is in great pain, having broken two ribs and suffered a punctured lung, but is uncomplaining. His trial is "very short and very clear": he is guilty. On the last day of the session, the judge picks Magwitch as a prime example of wickedness. Magwitch responds briefly but with dignity. "My Lord," he says, "I have received my sentence of Death from the Almighty, but I bow to yours."

On his last visit Pip finds his benefactor on his deathbed. As the old man is dying, Pip tells him that his daughter is alive. "She lived

48

and found powerful friends. She is living now. She is a lady and very beautiful. And I love her!" Magwitch raises Pip's hand to his lips, and dies.

Commentary

These chapters wind up the complicated plot element of the novel. Dickens is famous for the intricacy of his plots and the major concern at the end of his novels is often the unraveling of all the complexities found in the novel. Thus we have the final attempted escape, the capture of Magwitch, Magwitch's final revenge on his enemy, and his death in prison.

Pip's change is further emphasized in these chapters. When he earlier expected "great expectations," he acted in an incorrigible manner towards Joe and Biddy. Now he has no hopes of great expectations from anyone, so his conduct will be motivated solely by his purer instincts. Thus we see why Dickens had Pip return the money. Had he kept Magwitch's money, he would have been obligated to remain by Magwitch's side. Now that he can expect absolutely nothing, the decision to remain by him redeems Pip in the reader's sight. And his view of Magwitch has also undergone a complete reversal. All of Magwitch's repugnance has disappeared and in "the hunted, wounded, shackled creature," Pip sees only a man who has "felt affectionately, gratefully, and generously" towards him "with a constancy through a series of years." Furthermore, he sees in the convict a loyalty that is sorely missing in his own relationship with Joe.

CHAPTERS 57-59

Summary

Pip, now seriously in debt, gives notice on his chambers and plans to sublet them until his lease runs out. However, he falls seriously ill. Two men come to arrest him for debt, but he is too sick to be moved. When he regains consciousness after weeks of delirium, he finds Joe taking care of him; Biddy sent him down as soon as they learned that Pip was ill.

As he grows stronger, Pip learns that Miss Havisham is dead. She left the bulk of her estate to Estella, but a codicil gives a "cool" four thousand pounds (the phraseology is Joe's) to Matthew Pocket because of Pip's "account of the said Matthew."

Pip's health returns, and Joe becomes more distant and formal, addressing Pip as "Sir" again. Then one morning Pip awakens and finds Joe gone and a letter on the table: "Not wishful to intrude I have departured fur you are well again dear Pip and will do better without Jo. P. S. Ever the best of friends." Inside the note is a receipt for the debt for which Pip had been arrested. Pip knows that he must return to the forge and talk with Joe. He also hopes he can persuade Biddy to marry his old friend.

Walking home slowly, still weakened, Pip is alarmed at not hearing Joe's hammer at the forge. The reason is soon apparent: this is Joe and Biddy's wedding day. Pip congratulates them both in the old kitchen and tells them he will never cease working until he repays Joe the money that kept him out of prison, but that this is only a fraction of his debt to them. He also hopes that they will have a child who "will sit in this chimney-corner, of a winter night, who may remind you of another little fellow gone out of it forever," and who will become a better man than he did.

Back in London, Pip sells everything and goes East to join Herbert, who soon returns to bring Clara back with him. When Pip finally works up to become the third partner, Clarriker tells Herbert how Pip bought his partnership. Their friendship undiminished, Pip begins to realize that the ineptitude he had seen long ago in Herbert had been in himself.

After eleven years, he revisits England and finds Joe and Biddy the same, but parents of a small son, whom they have named Pip, and a daughter. When Biddy asks whether Pip still frets for Estella, he replies that this has all gone by. Nevertheless, after dinner he walks over to the cleared space that was once Satis House. He has heard that Estella, having been cruelly used, separated from Drummle, who was subsequently killed in "an accident consequent on his ill-treatment of a horse." The stars are shining and as Pip looks where the old house was, he sees a solitary figure beside a desolate garden walk: it is Estella.

The Satis House property, the last thing she held on to, is about to be built on, she explains, and she has come to bid it good-bye. Suffering has taught her much. She begs that they may be friends, even if apart.

"I took her hand in mine," Pip concludes, "and we went out of the ruined place; and, as the morning mists had risen long ago when I first left the forge, so the evening mists were rising now, and in all the broad expanse of tranquil light they showed to me, I saw no shadow of another parting from her."

Commentary

The final chapters of most Victorian novels are usually devoted to tidying up the narrative's loose ends and informing the reader of the disposition of all of the characters. *Great Expectations* is no exception. After Joe again demonstrates his generous nature, a true reconciliation is effected between Pip and Joe and Biddy. After the years of unhappiness between Joe and Mrs. Joe, he has now made a good marriage with Biddy. Herbert and Clara are also married, and Pip, after eleven years in the East, returns to England, meets Estella at Satis House, and realizes that she has been disciplined by life and made into a worthier person. In the "standard edition" ending, Pip sees "the shadow of no parting from her." This ending was written at the suggestion of one of Dickens' friends as being more appropriate for the reading public. In the original ending, Pip meets Estella in London and sees that she is greatly changed. She left Drummle and, after his death, married a doctor. They exchange gentle words with each other and then part forever. Dickens described the change this way: "I have put in as pretty a little piece of writing as I could, and I have no doubt the story will be more acceptable through the alteration."

CRITICAL ANALYSIS

THEME

The basic theme of *Great Expectations* is that true goodness does not come from social station or wealth; it comes from inner worth. Joe and Biddy illustrate this; so does Abel Magwitch. Pip has to learn it the hard way. His salvation is that, for all his ignorance during the days when he is a gentleman with great expectations, he finally does learn. Estella learns the hard way too, in both of Dickens' endings for this novel. One of the virtues of the original ending, however, is that it shows Pip as having discovered that one of the prices of finding his own worth is giving up his illusions.

For Dickens, a necessary corollary to this basic theme was that wealth and position are corrupting. He has been severely criticized for hypocrisy about this view—a charge that a man who was writing a novel to save his own magazine and to preserve his comfortable existence as the squire of Gad's Hill obviously left himself open to. Despite his few early years of hardship, Dickens never personally turned his back on wealth and position. George Orwell, the author of *1984*, states the case very strongly; Dickens' real allegiance, he says, was to the "shabby genteel."

The trouble with this view is that it confuses the man with the book. Regardless of Dickens' personal habits, there is no doubt of what he was trying to say in *Great Expectations*. The good people are for the most part the working people and the rebels. Joe Gargery and Abel Magwitch, different as they are, both epitomize this. It is no accident that Compeyson, Magwitch's great enemy, passes for a gentleman while Magwitch is a "warmint."

It is very easy to oversimplify all this. In fact, critics have made a career of oversimplifying Dickens. There are ambiguities throughout the novel. Magwitch, convict and rebel that he is, spends—and loses—his life trying to make Pip a gentleman. Orlick, a journeyman blacksmith, is a villain. Herbert Pocket, poor but genteel, is a naturally good man. The point is that Dickens wrote about *people*, some of them good, some of them bad. It is also, however, important to understand the general drift of his sympathies without falling into the error of assuming that he wrote a tract rather than a novel.

This brings us back to the reasons for Dickens' success as a popular novelist. We have already noted that part of the reason was his enormous skill at characterization and plot structure. But this was only part of it. The other ingredient was his universal theme, exemplified in this novel as in all his others. Dickens was no social reformer, though much paper has been used up in analyzing him in these terms. He had passionate convictions about many social questions and a passionate hatred of such institutions as courts, jails, and the law in general. But these feelings stemmed from a much more fundamental point of view.

Dickens was a sentimental, complicated man with strong moral feelings which he frequently failed to live up to himself. His formal schooling was very limited, as was his knowledge of literature, the arts, and a considerable segment of English society—the upper classes. Note that during the whole of Pip's career in London learning to become a gentleman, we never see him actually engaged in any "gentlemanly" activities, unless the dinner with the Finches of the Grove, which is only a pretext for an encounter with Drummle, can be termed such. But what Dickens did know—the life of the common man in London, the plight of those who fall afoul of the law, and how life was for the ordinary man in the country villages—he knew accurately.

But his readers also understood something else. Stripped to its essentials, the moral structure of this private world could almost be described as a Victorian melodrama. It was Good versus Evil, the honest and loyal man against the selfish schemer. His audience reveled in this, just as today's American audiences revel nightly in cowboy, detective, and similar shows on television. And this is intended as no slur on Dickens. This antithesis is the basis of the greater part of literature. What matters is how it is treated. If in Dickens the lines were generally sharper, the opposites simpler and more clear cut, he nevertheless used this polarity as a vehicle for his characterization, his plot structure, and his style.

PLOT STRUCTURE

To understand Dickens' incredible skill at this complicated art, we must understand his method of composition. From the beginning, Dickens wrote for publication in periodicals for a very simple reason. This is where the quickest money was, and Dickens always, like many writers, needed quick money, "portable property," in Wemmick's favorite phrase. However, serialization in Dickens' time was utterly unlike the same thing today. The author would often end his narrative for the magazine upon what was called a "cliff-hanger"—that is, the end of a magazine episode would end in such a manner as to cause the reading public to anxiously await the next edition of the magazine to discover "what happened." For example, at the end of Chapter 4, when Mrs. Joe misses the pork pie and is wondering about its theft, there is a knock at the door and when Pip answers the door, he is confronted with a constable holding out a pair of handcuffs. The implication is that Pip has been discovered as the thief. The reader, however, must wait until the next edition of the magazine to discover what has happened. In this way the magazine was insured a continued circulation. Nowadays, an author often finishes a book first and then sells the serial rights. Dickens, in contrast, stayed just one jump ahead of his deadlines, so that most of the book would be in print before the final chapter had even been written.

In spite of this, his plot structure in this novel is impeccable. As has been noted in the comments on individual chapters, all the basic plot lines have been set out by the end of Chapter 11, and the principal characters have appeared on stage. This is a remarkable achievement for any author; for a man who was rushing serial chapters into print, it is truly incredible.

STYLE

There is no part of Dickens' art, especially in the later novels, that has been less appreciated than his ability as a stylist. This is better illustrated than simply commented on. A suitable example is this one from Chapter 45, where Pip is staying at Hummums after Wemmick's warning: "Don't Go Home."

"There was an inhospitable smell in the room of cold soot and hot dust; and, as I looked up into the corners of the tester over my head, I thought what a number of bluebottle flies from the butcher's, and earwigs from the market, and grubs from the country, must be holding on up there, lying by for next summer. This led me to speculate whether any of them ever tumbled down, and then I fancied that I felt light falls on my face—a disagreeable turn of thought, suggesting other and more objectionable approaches up my back. When I had lain awake a little while, those extraordinary voices with which silence teems began to make themselves audible. The closet whispered, the fireplace sighed, the little washing-stand ticked, and one guitar-string played occasionally in the chest of drawers. At about the same time, the eyes on the wall acquired a new expression, and in every one of those staring rounds I saw written, DON'T GO HOME.''

The point about this kind of writing is not simply Dickens' marvelously precise use of words. The important thing is that Dickens transcends this precision. He manages to make the physical scene a part of the psychological experience of the person involved. Pip's inner fears and confusions are described in terms of the *furniture*. This goes beyond the standard novelistic technique of identifying a person's role and station by the kind of surroundings he chooses to have around him.

SOCIAL CRITICISM

So much has been written about Dickens as a social critic that one sometimes feels such commentators have forgotten that he was a novelist, not a reformer. He had, as we have earlier noted, passionate convictions about many social matters, and these constantly recur in his novels. But he had no interest in plunging himself into the committed and demanding life of the reformer. He was much more interested in writing, in acting and its offshoot, his readings, and in living the good life as the Squire of Gad's Hill. His social concerns were a part of his general moral concern, but only a part, and we misread him if we try to separate the social protest out from the whole. Fagin's mistreatment of Oliver in *Oliver Twist* and Mrs. Joe's mistreatment of Pip in *Great Expectations* are, in human terms, the same. It is people that Dickens is primarily interested in.

Consider the law and the penal system, Dickens' prime targets for social criticism in *Great Expectations*. Without question he gives them their come-uppance, even going out of his way (in Chapter 32) to get Pip inside Newgate, at the same time utilizing this diversion with his customary skill to juxtapose Estella with the life of crime Pip believes her to be so remote from. But what he is really interested in is the remarkable characters involved in this process—Jaggers, Wemmick, and Magwitch. It is not correct to call his social criticisms incidental, but they *are* secondary.

In passing, it is worth noting that Dickens was not really writing about his own day at all. By 1860, for example, the railroad age was well advanced in England, but in *Great Expectations* the standard means of travel is by coach.

CHARACTER ANALYSES

With the possible exceptions of Dostoevsky and Faulkner, there has been no writer of fiction in the Western world who had Dickens' genius for creating such an infinite variety of characters. Part of this, of course, is a result of the sheer bulk of his work, but primarily it is a tribute to his inventiveness. Characters sprang from Dickens' mind full-blown, like Athena from the brow of Zeus. One of the hardest jobs for a writer of a guide to Dickens' novels is to keep the discussion of characters within reasonable bounds. The problem is not merely that there are so many of them; it is that they are all so interesting.

It was this ability, plus his amazing aptitude for plot structure, which in part accounted for his enormous success as a popular novelist. The point that many of his critics have missed, however, is that all these people, no matter how briefly sketched, are *real*. They are generally outlined with very clear characteristics—Jaggers, for example, points with his great forefinger, buries his nose in his handkerchief, apparently equivocates, but moves ruthlessly to the end of whatever business he is about. Nevertheless, there is also a great subtlety in the depiction of Jaggers. His kindness to Estella, Molly, Miss Havisham, and Pip, for example, does not fit the stereotype Dickens first seems to have made of him.

As a result, Dickens put more enduring characters into the minds of English and American readers than any writer since Shakespeare. This alone would insure his greatness.

Pip (Philip Pirrip)

One of the most interesting things about Pip is that he is the only character in the novel of whom we have no physical description whatever. Dickens was a master of quick characterization through appearance, but we never learn what Pip looks like.

There is nothing accidental about this. What Dickens is interested in is Pip's *interior*. His concern is the changes that take place inside Pip. Dickens' usual habit is to give his characters sharply marked physical characteristics which reflect their moral attitudes. Generally they stay in character throughout. Pip does none of these things. He changes, radically: he moves from a frightened and selfish innocence, to the snobbery and pretense of being a manufactured gentleman, to the wisdom that the convict Magwitch's basic goodness finally forces on him.

The external facts of Pip's life are very simple, despite the series of dramatic episodes he participates in. An orphan who never saw his parents, for reasons which are not explained, he is raised "by hand" by his sister, Mrs. Joe Gargery, befriended by her husband, the village blacksmith, and begins his career by finding a convict, Abel Magwitch, on the marshes one morning when he has gone out to visit his parents' graves. This sets off a series of events which includes his association with Miss Havisham and his fascination by Estella, his great expectations, which he finally learns have been provided by Magwitch, and his eventual discovery, after Magwitch's capture and death, that his convict was one of the five genuinely good people he has ever known. The others are Biddy, Joe Gargery, Herbert Pocket, and John Wemmick. The point of the novel is that Pip himself finally becomes a good man.

Miss Havisham

We never learn her first name. She is the daughter of a wealthy brewer; her brother Arthur, a ne'er-do-well, has conspired with the book's villain, Compeyson, to swindle her through a fraudulent engagement. When Compeyson does not show up for the wedding, Miss Havisham stops all the clocks in the house at the precise time his letter of regret arrived, twenty minutes to nine, and spends the rest of her life in her yellowed bridal gown, wearing only one shoe because she had not yet put on the other at the time of the disaster, and educating Estella, her adopted daughter, to wreak her revenge on men.

At the time Pip first meets her, she is a gaunt, white-haired woman with wild eyes. She remains this to the end. She undergoes a superficial change, but, unlike Pip's, it is not a real one. What she discovers is remorse when she finds that she has made Estella into a girl with a heart of ice. But this too is in character. She has always been an utterly self-centered person, and her dismay about Estella reflects her realization of the fact that by making the girl unable to love, she has made her unable to love *her*. She is undoubtedly insane, and in a well-regulated modern world would have been committed long ago. Dickens' readers can be thankful that in Victorian England, eccentrics, as they were then called, were left alone as long as they stayed indoors. Miss Havisham did, and died there. But she remains one of the most enduring characters in the novel.

Joe Gargery

Joe is a rather incredible characterization. Any writer knows that it is much easier to depict bad people than good ones: bad people are generally more complicated and therefore more interesting. A standard critical commentary on Milton's *Paradise Lost*, for example, is that Lucifer is the most interesting character in the poem. Nevertheless, Joe, a rough giant who is unalloyed goodness, is one of the most alive characters Dickens ever created.

Joe grew up the son of a lovable but drunken father and had to quit school to support his mother. Until he married Biddy, he never learned to read or write. But he has great native intelligence, as well as formidable skills as a blacksmith. He considers himself simple, but his conversation, which Dickens renders impeccably, shows him to be just the opposite. He is whole-hearted, a considerably different thing. He submits to Mrs. Joe's rampages because he feels an obligation to be good to women, and because he would rather have her wrath fall on him than on Pip. He is, in his own words, "ever the best of friends" with Pip—a man to cherish.

Abel Magwitch

Magwitch, besides being central to the book, is also one of its most interesting characters. Unlike Joe, his image is ambiguous. Superficially he seems all bad. Most of his life he has been a prisoner or a convict; he is the latter throughout the novel. When Pip first encountered him on the marshes, he was "a fearful man, all in coarse gray, with a great iron on his leg." When Magwitch arrives in London years later, to inform Pip, in his new guise as "Provis," that he has been his benefactor, Pip finds him equally revolting and refuses, foolishly, to take anything from him.

Underneath, however, Abel Magwitch is a tender and generous man. The father of Estella, the husband of Molly (Jaggers' housekeeper), the enemy of Compeyson, and the creator of Pip's great expectations, Magwitch dies, denounced by the law (Chapter 56) but beloved by his foster son, Pip.

Estella Havisham

Estella has had a hard and undeserved time at the hands of critics. She becomes precisely what Miss Havisham educated her to be—a girl with a heart of ice. But she also, as she grows up, develops a basic honesty that is admirable. In contrast to her treatment of Pip as a child, when she had called him a common laboring-boy with coarse hands and thick boots, she tries to explain to him that emotion is something she is incapable of feeling. She says the same thing to Miss Havisham. The fact that neither of them understands her is evidence of their illusions, not her cruelty.

Estella is beautiful and intelligent, and she becomes a lady. She marries a boor, Drummle, out of malice aforethought. "Should I fling myself away," she tells Pip (Chapter 44) "on the man who would the soonest feel (if people do feel such things) that I took nothing to him?" That man would have been Pip, even though, he cannot understand it. But Estella's honesty, in these situations, is a part of her ironic heritage from her father, Abel Magwitch, a convict, and her mother, Molly, a murderess. What Dickens is trying to say through Estella is that a potentially good woman has been warped through a pseudo-aristocratic education grounded in hate.

Molly

We learn very little about Molly except the details of her crime: she murdered an older woman out of jealousy over Magwitch, and Jaggers got her off; she became Jaggers' housekeeper immediately afterwards, a wild beast whom the lawyer tamed; she is also Estella's mother. Her resemblance to Estella makes Pip eventually realize that she is indeed Estella's mother. Her chief physical characteristic is her immensely strong wrists.

Mr. Jaggers

In a novel full of strong characters, he is one of the strongest. He is burly, has a great forefinger which he is always aiming at people while he is making a point, often gestures with a large silk handkerchief which he employs any time he needs to stall, and he washes frequently with scented soap.

He is also perhaps the most intelligent man in the book. Jaggers is the epitome of the shrewd, arrogant, and careful lawyer. He never commits himself to anything, and he is apparently interested only in things which will make money for him. But he also saves Estella from a foredoomed criminal career, takes in Molly when the easiest thing would have been to forget about her, and treats Pip with a kindness which this young man is not at the time equipped to understand.

Dickens hated the courts and lawyers. His trouble with Jaggers was that he fell in love with his own creation. Undoubtedly he started out to make Jaggers a parody of all the parts of the law that he hated. But Jaggers got too big to be a parody and became a man in his own right—a transformation for which we should all be grateful.

Uncle Pumblechook

Of all the distasteful characters that Dickens ever created, Pumblechook is a good candidate for the top of the list. He is the classic humbug. Through him Dickens, again speaking for the underprivileged, is saying that the small-time operator who has hustled his way to success in a little business can be depended on to be untruthful. Pumblechook represents that subsection of the rising middle class that Dickens particularly detested. Pumblechook, a corn and seed merchant, thinks he has helped Pip achieve his great expectations and fawns over Pip, but runs him down to everyone when Pip does not show proper "gratitude." Actually, he had no hand in Pip's good fortune.

John Wemmick

He is one of the novel's genuinely good people. He, too, is carefully typed, but in two roles. The "London Wemmick" is absolutely precise, has a mouth like "a postbox," and follows the coldly businesslike methods he has learned from his master, Jaggers. The "Walworth Wemmick" is relaxed, gentle, and completely devoted to his father, the "Aged Parent." As his home, he has constructed an imitation castle with a moat a few feet wide, and a cannon, the Stinger, which Wemmick fires every night at precisely nine because it's the only thing the Aged can hear.

With Pip, Wemmick breaks the dichotomy of his existence to give him Walworth help in London. He also invites Pip to his marriage, in one of the most charming chapters of the book (Chapter 55). He is the source, unwittingly, of the misinformation that leads to Magwitch's capture.

Mr. Wopsle

While it is not correct to say that any of Dickens' characters has no function in the plot—he puts them all to work—Wopsle comes close. A former parish clerk with a fine voice and ambitions for the stage, Wopsle grows steadily in Dickens' mind all through the story. At first he is only a spear carrier: his function is to provide comic relief in the small society of Pip's unnamed village. Later, having become a London actor under the name of "Mr. Waldengarver," a mediocre Hamlet and buffoon, he serves as the means of alerting Pip to the fact that Compeyson is tailing him.

REVIEW QUESTIONS

1. How does the atmosphere and setting in the early chapters of the novel enhance the emotional states of the orphan and the convict?

2. How is Joe's profession as a blacksmith initially important to the plot?

3. How does Dickens suggest a measure of sympathy for Magwitch when we first encounter him?

4. Discuss the "victimization" theme, in regard to Magwitch, Joe, and Pip.

5. How would the novel change if Pip refused to help Magwitch?

6. Discuss the hostility between Magwitch and Compeyson.

7. How does Magwitch return Pip's goodness?

8. What is Magwitch's sentence after he is apprehended?

9. Why is Estella so cold to Pip?

10. Describe Miss Havisham and her house.

11. Why is Pip so fascinated by Estella?

12. What role does Matthew Pocket play in Pip's growing up?

13. Who is the "pale young gentleman" whom Pip meets and what particular quality does Pip discern about him?

14. Discuss Miss Havisham's relatives and her attitude towards them.

15. Why does Pip believe that Miss Havisham is probably his benefactor?

16. What is Orlick's role in the novel? Why are he and Pip antagonistic to one another?

17. Why does Biddy move into Mrs. Joe's household?

18. Why does Pip treat Joe so snobbishly?

19. What sort of lawyer is Jaggers? What is his relationship with Pip?

20. Describe Pip's first impression of London.

21. How does Dickens arouse and sustain our interest in Molly, Jaggers' housekeeper?

22. What is the function of Dickens' depiction of Newgate Prison in the novel?

23. What is the irony of Pip's thinking of Estella as superior to the Newgate setting?

24. Describe Pip's generosity in regard to Herbert Pocket; be specific.

25. What is Pip's reaction when he discovers the true identity of his benefactor?

26. Where and why in the narrative line does Dickens insert mention of Magwitch's "missis" and Compeyson?

27. How is Pip rescued from Orlick?

28. Describe Miss Havisham's last months.

29. How is she involved in Herbert's future?

30. What happens to Compeyson?

31. Discuss Pip's reconciliation with Joe and Biddy.

32. Which of Dickens' endings for *Great Expectations* do you prefer and why?

33. Discuss Dickens' use of either humor or irony in the novel.

34. What is the moral lesson of the novel?

35. What is your favorite episode in the novel? Find examples and details of style and characterization that make the episode effective.

SELECTED BIBLIOGRAPHY

Chesterton, Gilbert Keith. *Charles Dickens*. New York: Schocken Books, 1965.

Engel, Monroe. *The Maturity of Dickens*. Cambridge, Massachusetts: Harvard University Press, 1959.

Fielding, K. J. *Charles Dickens: A Critical Introduction*. New York: David McKay Co., 1958.

Forster, John. *The Life of Charles Dickens*, 2 vols. New York: E. P. Dutton, 1928.

Gissing, George. *Critical Studies of the Works of Charles Dickens*. New York, Greenberg, 1924.

House, Humphry. *The Dickens World*, 2nd ed. New York: Oxford University Press, 1960.

Huxley, Aldous. *Vulgarity in Literature*. London: Chatto and Windus, 1930.

Johnson, Edgar. *Charles Dickens: His Tragedy and Triumph*, 2 vols. New York: Simon and Schuster, 1953. (The standard biography).

Leacock, Stephen. *Charles Dickens: His Life and Work*. Garden City, New York: Doubleday, Doran, 1934.

Ley, J. W. T. *The Dickens Circle*. London: Chapman and Hall, 1919.

Miller, J. Hillis. *Charles Dickens: The World of His Novels*. Cambridge, Massachusetts: Harvard University Press, 1959.

Nisbet, Ada. *Dickens and Ellen Ternan*. Berkeley: University of California Press, 1952.

Orwell, George. *Dickens, Dali and Others*. New York: Harcourt, Brace, 1946.

Pearson, Hesketh. *Dickens: His Character, Comedy, and Career*. New York: Harper and Brothers, 1949.

Pope-Hennessy, Una. *Charles Dickens: 1812-1870*. London: Howell, Soskin, 1946.

Van Ghent, Dorothy. *The English Novel: Form and Function*. New York: Holt, Rinehart and Winston, 1953.

Wilson, Edmund. *The Wound and the Bow*. New York: Oxford University Press, 1947.

NOTES

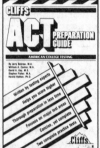